BRUCE TEGNER'S
COMPLETE BOOK OF
SELF-DEFENSE

is the first lesson plan available in book form. It is similar to those Mr. Tegner has prepared for police and army courses. It includes over 400 photographs, four progress tests, a chart showing the pressure points of the body where blows are most effective, and a complete reference index of blows, locks and other techniques. It also includes special instructions on how you can teach your child, your wife or your friends the arts of self-defense.

D1002783

BRUCE TEGNER'S
COMPLETE BOOK
OF SELF-DEFENSE

BANTAM BOOKS
TORONTO · NEW YORK · LONDON

*This low-priced Bantam Book
has been completely reset in a type face
designed for easy reading, and was printed
from new plates. It contains the complete
text of the original hard-cover edition.*
NOT ONE WORD HAS BEEN OMITTED.

BRUCE TEGNER'S COMPLETE BOOK OF SELF-DEFENSE
*A Bantam Book / published by arrangement with
Stein and Day, Publishers*

PRINTING HISTORY
Stein and Day edition published May 1963
Bantam edition published January 1965

2nd printing .... February 1965	5th printing .... December 1966
3rd printing ...... August 1965	6th printing .... May 1967
4th printing ... September 1966	7th printing .... March 1968

8th printing

9th printing

10th printing

ACKNOWLEDGMENTS
*The author wishes to thank Jacques Bellesiles and
Glen Rankel for assisting him in demonstrating
the techniques in the photos in the main body
of this book. Richard Tarnutzer and Tevis F.
Morrow, Jr., show the work in the children's
section. Alice McGrath shows the techniques
in the section for women.*

*This manuscript was prepared under the
supervision of Alice McGrath.*

This book is dedicated to DANIEL SCHECHTER.

Published simultaneously in the United States and Canada

Bantam Books are published by Bantam Books, Inc., a subsidiary
of Grosset & Dunlap, Inc. Its trade-mark, consisting of the words
"Bantam Books" and the portrayal of a bantam, is registered in the
United States Patent Office and in other countries. Marca Registrada.
Bantam Books, Inc., 271 Madison Avenue, New York, N.Y. 10016.

PRINTED IN THE UNITED STATES OF AMERICA

About Bruce Tegner

Bruce Tegner is regarded as the most experienced instructor in America in the arts of unarmed self-defense. As the son of two American Judo instructors (*both* his parents were Black Belt holders) he was brought up under the tutelage of Oriental and European masters of the unarmed arts and actually began his formal training when he was two years old. His training covered all the different types of unarmed fighting . . . a most unusual background in an area where specialized training was the tradition. By the time he was fifteen Mr. Tegner was already a professional instructor and at seventeen he achieved the rank of Second Black Belt . . . then the youngest American to receive this honor.

Mr. Tegner served in the armed forces of the United States as an instructor in charge of training teachers of Judo and Karate for the regular Army, Military Police, Marines, and special Ranger units.

After leaving the Army Mr. Tegner continued to improve his teaching methods with the aim of perfecting a system which would be most useful for Americans.

Mr. Tegner has taught professionally since 1945 and since 1952 has had his own school in Hollywood where he has taught thousands of men, women, and children.

In addition to work at his own school, Mr. Tegner has devised a special course of instruction used by law enforcement agencies throughout the country and has been employed by the United States government to instruct border-patrol personnel and Treasury agents. Movie and TV studios frequently call upon him for expert technical advice.

Introduction

For many years the arts of self-defense were kept the secret of a small group of teachers and students who did not wish the general public to learn them. In order to accomplish this they developed a mysterious, difficult, and, in many cases, boring teaching procedure in which the student spent arduous months learning the simplest techniques and was forced to practice them numberless times before moving on to new ones.

I was brought up under this Oriental method of teaching and have come to realize how unsatisfactory it is for the American student of self-defense.

The old style of training, still followed by many instructors, demands an Oriental-way-of-life approach which is rooted in feudal Asia and is totally inappropriate today. Incredible as it may seem, some traditional schools still teach a technique meant for the sole purpose of crashing through Samurai armor.

These ritual oriented teachers prefer to perpetuate the traditional harsh methods of instruction instead of trying to modernize and popularize the unarmed arts. Thus they prevent any but the most exceptional student from succeeding in his training.

However, in many ways it is more important to encourage the least, rather than the most, skillful to participate in physical activity. So it is with the unarmed arts. The timid, fearful child needs self-defense instruction much more than the hardy, vigorous child, and the enrichment of life which accompanies the learning and accomplishment that can be found through this book is most useful to those who lack confidence and self-esteem. Such people are the least likely to survive the "proving" period of the traditional method of training.

A second great defect of the old style of teaching is that it is based on a specific defense for each specific attack, and since there are literally thousands of ways of making attacks, thousands of different defenses had to be learned. The period required to learn the many defense "tricks" made it impossible to learn anything at all practical in less than several years of study. What I have done in my school and have now put down in this book is to develop a method which is useful in *types* of situations, rather than in *specific* situations. Thus, a small number of techniques taught in a short time will achieve the same result as years of training in the old-fashioned way. Because of this a student who has trained for a month with my method may be much better prepared than a student of the traditional style who has trained for a year. Other modifications and modernizations which I have introduced to make the ancient arts serve us better for our present-day needs are explained throughout the text.

This book has been many years in preparation. The techniques which are described are the result of years of testing and selection and are the same that you would receive as a student in my school.

In teaching thousands of men, women, and children, I have seen them grow in many other ways besides in their ability to defend themselves. I hope that this course will give you, as it has given them, a new sense of achievement and confidence, of power and dignity.

BRUCE TEGNER

Contents

THE THIRD DAY

THE FOURTH DAY

THE FIFTH DAY

First Progress Test

THE SIXTH DAY

THE SEVENTH DAY

THE EIGHTH DAY

THE NINTH DAY

THE TENTH DAY

THE TWELFTH DAY

THE THIRTEENTH DAY

THE FOURTEENTH DAY

Falls No. 1, 2, 3, 6, 7
Front-Choke Defenses No. 3 and 4
Arm-Pin Defense—Back Attack
Fist-Fighting Defense—Close-In Attack—
  Block and Simultaneous Blows with Take-down
  Parry and Forward Trip
Knife Defense—Stabbing Attack
Straight-Leg Throw—Throwing and Receiving
Sitting-Down Throw—(Position Only)

NEW INSTRUCTION:

THE FIFTEENTH DAY

Falls No. 1, 2, 3, 7, 8
Arm-Pin Defense—Back Attack
Back-Grab Defense—Under Arms
Reverse Arm Lock
Finger Pressure and Arm Lock
Fist-Fighting Defense—Parry and Forward Trip
Knife Defense—Stabbing and Slashing Attacks
Straight-Leg Throw—Throwing and Receiving
Sitting-Down Throw—Throwing and Receiving

NEW INSTRUCTION:

Third Progress Test

THE SIXTEENTH DAY

Falls No. 1, 2, 3, 7, 8
Over-Arm Lock
Arm-Pin Defense—Back Attack

Back-Grab Defense—Under Arms
Close-In Fist-Fighting Defense—Block, Leap, Kick,
   and Choke
Knife Defense—Stabbing and Slashing Attacks
Straight-Leg Throw—Throwing and Receiving
Sitting-Down Throw—Throwing and Receiving
Circle Throw—(Position Only)

NEW INSTRUCTION:

THE SEVENTEENTH DAY

Falls No. 1, 2, 3, 7, 8
Fist-Fighting Defense:
   Hip-Throw Ending
   Swinging-Leg-Throw Ending
Close-In Fist-Fighting Defense—Block, Leap, Kick,
   and Choke
Knife Defense—Stabbing and Slashing Attacks
Back-Grab Defense—Over Arms
Gang-Attack Defense—Front and Back
Sitting-Down Throw—Throwing and Receiving
Circle Throw—Throwing and Receiving

NEW INSTRUCTION:

THE EIGHTEENTH DAY

Falls No. 1, 2, 3, 7, 9
Wrist-Grab Defense —All Four Types
Grab Defense—Thumb Release and Arm Lock
Over-Arm Lock
Bent-Arm Lock—Rear
Knife Defense—Threat of Attack
Circle Throw—Throwing and Receiving
Sweeping-Foot Throw—(Position Only)

NEW INSTRUCTION:

THE NINETEENTH DAY

THE TWENTIETH DAY

THE TWENTY-FIRST DAY

Fourth Progress Test

Preliminary Instruction

In beginning your practice sessions, you and your partner should not resist each other, or try to avoid the defense techniques. At first you will be learning the *form* of the techniques, and it does not help either your learning process or your partner's to offer resistance, or to attempt to outwit him.

Beginners must think of themselves as beginners. A driving instructor does not take you for your first lesson onto a busy freeway, but starts the learning process on a deserted street. As your skill increases, he will allow you to drive into moderate traffic and then into heavy traffic as you learn to handle the situation. The same is true of this training. It would be foolish for you to expect to learn any technique so well during the first few days that you could execute it properly and swiftly against actual attack. You should start without any resistance from your partner. As you make progress, your partner may offer some opposition. As you make further progress, he should offer more resistance until you are able to execute a technique without his cooperation.

Eventually you will achieve the skill, quick reaction, speed of execution, and control of power which makes the defense effective on the street.

BY THE NUMBERS

You will learn best if you follow the training plan exactly as it is presented. First, do the techniques in slow motion and by the numbers. Study the photographs and compare them with what you are doing. Correct any mistakes you make before going on. Work along from photo to photo, carefully and slowly.

When you thoroughly understand the "pieces" of each defense, you may begin to perform them still slowly and without hesitation as a single continuous motion. Your aim should be a smooth and accurate technique.

When you can perform a technique properly and smoothly, you will be ready to increase your speed as well. Do not rush through the first part of learning any technique, or you will omit the solid foundation of knowledge which is essential to develop your skill fully.

BASIC STANCES

The natural stance is a relaxed standing position. Your feet are shoulder-width apart and your weight is distributed equally on both feet. In the natural stance you will have strong balance from side to side. That is, if you were pushed from the side you would have strong resistance to the push. However, in this stance you will have poor balance to resist a push from either the front or the back.

The "T" position gives you the strongest balance position that you can assume. In the "T" position you are stronger from side to side and from front to back than in any other stance. If you are right-handed, your "T" stance is with your right foot pointing straight forward and your left foot pointing to the side. Your knees should be bent slightly, and your weight distributed equally on both feet. Among its advantages, the "T" position places the side of your body toward your opponent and thereby offers him less target area. It also places you in position for delivering effective foot blows. If you are left-handed, your "T" position will be with your left foot pointing forward.

One point balance

When all your weight is on one foot you are in the weakest possible position. As you progress in the course, you will learn to avoid placing yourself in this vulnerable position and to take advantage of this weakness when your opponent has done so.

FIGHTING STANCES

The fighting stances are strong, balanced, protective, ready positions. In a fighting stance, you are obviously prepared for action. If, because of it, your adversary is persuaded to back down, so much the better. If he requires the persuasion of physical action, you can move quickly from it.

"T" position: your left hand is ready to slash or block. Your right hand is ready to deliver a knuckle blow.

Typical Karate fighting stance: "T" position. Your left hand is in a low blocking position, your right hand is in position to deliver an edge-of-the-hand blow. This is a useful stance when confronted by a crouching adversary.

When practicing the techniques in this course that involve blocking and striking, start with the defending partner in a fighting stance.

NATURAL AND UNNATURAL GRIP

When you are instructed to grip with a **natural grip**, reach forward as though to shake hands, as shown in the photo above. Whether you are gripping cloth or a hand, the position is the same.

When you are instructed to grip with an **unnatural grip**, reach forward, as shown by the partner at the right. In this position your hand is turned over so that the thumb points down and the palm is facing out.

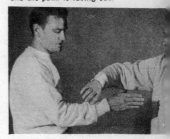

"T" position: Hands in conventional boxing on-guard. The "T" position gives you strong balance, and the hand position does not reveal the manner in which you intend to strike.

LENGTH OF PRACTICE SESSIONS

Obviously the more time you can give to each practice session and the greater the frequency of the sessions, the quicker you will master the techniques. As a general rule you should plan to spend one hour covering the techniques in each day's lesson. After the third lesson you can practice by yourself between the sessions of work with your partner.

You will make good progress whether the sessions with your partner are two days or a week apart. It is best not to try to rush through the lessons. Patient and steady work will accomplish more than rapid half-learning.

SAFETY

Tapping your partner, the ground or yourself is the signal for submission. The first and most important safety rule is to release your partner as soon as he signals. The techniques which you are learning in this course have been effective for many thousands of years and you are not trying to prove that they work. It does not help you or your partner if you inflict pain during the practice sessions. Tapping is preferable to a verbal signal because it is more definite and because, sometimes, as in chokes, it is easier to tap than to talk.

Chokes must be practiced lightly. Experiment on yourself and you will see how little pressure is needed to cause discomfort. Slight finger pressure on the windpipe or the throat hollow is painful and if you dig your fingers lightly into your own neck you will understand the effectiveness of heavier pressure.

Hand and foot blows should be practiced without hurting your partner. Touch lightly in beginning practice and learn to pull your blows as you progress. If you wish to deliver moderate blows in your practice, you may improvise padding for shins and forearms by using towels or other materials. If you use padding, fasten it with bandage clamps or adhesive tape. Do not use pins. Heavy blows should be practiced only against the sawdust bag.

Locks and holds must be practiced with a smooth, slow action. Avoid snappy, jerky motions for locks and holds. As you acquire skill, you will be able to execute the holds and locks with increasing speed and yet maintain control and not hurt your partner. Be alert for your partner's signal of submission, and release instantly at the first tap.

THROWING PRACTICE

Throwing can be learned thoroughly and with complete safety when you follow these directions exactly:

Start your practice of all throws in slow motion. Skill, not speed, is essential. Speed will come to you easily when you have acquired skill.

When you start your training, you may practice to the point of executing the throw, without actually throwing. For this practice, you can work on any surface. When you proceed to the actual throwing action, you must work on a cushioned surface. A grass lawn or a sandy beach will do if you do not have a gym or Judo mats at your disposal. Even when you are in the "easing down" stage of learning the throws, you will need a cushioned surface for safety.

An experienced student, of course, can fall properly without hurting himself on the hard surface of a wood floor or even on cement.

HAND CONDITIONING

Excessive toughening of the hand results in a deformed appearance and is not required for practical self-defense. If your hands are very sensitive and you wish to toughen them moderately, soak them in salt water for a few minutes each day.

COORDINATION AND ACCURACY EXERCISE

Since you are depending on skill rather than on power for the success of the techniques which you will learn in this course, you will greatly increase your proficiency by developing accuracy, coordination, and balance. One way to do this is to work with a moving target. You can make one in the following way: Using a solid rubber ball about three inches in diameter, force a cord through the center —an ice pick will normally do the job—and tie a knot to secure it. Suspend the ball where it can swing freely—a door jamb indoors, or a tree out of doors—passing the cord through an eyelet screw so that you can vary the height of the ball.

Suspend the ball so that it is at your knee height. Practice kicking it, first with one foot and then with the other. In the beginning, use only a single kick in the following manner:

Stand facing the ball. Pivot on your right foot so that the side of your body is toward the ball. Lean the top part of your body back, draw your left leg up, and kick the ball with the bottom of your left foot. Immediately after kicking place your left foot on the ground so that you regain your balance.

Repeat the kick with your right foot, this time pivoting on your left foot. Alternate single kicks several times. When you can kick well in this manner, you may proceed to practice two or more kicks consecutively. In the beginning you may have difficulty kicking the ball more than two times consecutively. You may gauge your progress by the increasing accuracy with which you can do the kicking exercises.

In a fight, no target will be as difficult to hit as the practice ball.

Suspend the small ball so that it is at your face height. Practice a variety of hand blows, using both hands for striking. Do not hit with force. The ball need only be swinging gently to give you adequate practice. In the beginning you may be able to hit the ball accurately only two or three times. As you progress, you should be able to increase the number of times you can hit the target, as well as change from one type of blow to another without effort.

With a moderate amount of this practice continued throughout the course, you will not only learn a variety of blows and find that you can hit easily with either hand, but you will also find that your general coordination has improved greatly.

27

HITTING WITH POWER

Most of us, even persons with a rather slight build, have enough power to hit with telling force by using the knowledge of where and how to strike to good effect.

Normally, we do not realize the amount of power we *do* possess, not having the opportunity to test it. Although it is more important to achieve accuracy and skill, it is wise to practice some full-power blows during the course of the training.

In the section *SAFETY* you will find directions for practicing moderately heavy blows with your partner. Full-power blows cannot be practiced this way for the same reason that you cannot use a friend for target practice with a loaded gun—it is too dangerous.

A heavy laundry bag or duffle bag filled with wood shavings or sawdust may be used to practice heavy blows. Suspend the bag with a strong rope or chain. (The bag will exert a heavy pull, so be certain that it is well anchored.)

Using the fleshy part of the edge of your hand, hit straight out at the bag. Take a short step forward as you strike. This will put your body weight behind the blow. You can feel the difference between the force delivered in this way and one that is not if you stand in a natural stance and hit the bag without taking the step.

Hit the bag with an edge-of-the-hand blow, taking a step as you hit. Follow up with a knuckle blow, using your other hand.

Hit the bag with an elbow blow, again taking a step forward as the blow is delivered.

Practice in order to develop a variety of blows which you can deliver with either hand. If you are right-handed, stress practice with your left hand to increase your skill.

Use the bag for practicing foot blows, stressing a variety of blows and alternating kicks with your right and your left foot. You must be able to strike these blows without losing your balance.

For self-defense in a street situation, low-and-middle-area kicks are most practical. In your practice session, you should train yourself to kick high as this will automatically give you the ability to kick low as well. Moreover, it is good practice and excellent exercise.

TROUBLE SPOTS AND SELECTION OF TECHNIQUES

As you progress, you will find some techniques which present a problem to you. They will be different for each individual, and work which is easy for one partner to learn may be difficult for the other partner.

The first few times you try any new technique it will seem strange and awkward. It is only after you have made considerable effort that you can determine those techniques which are suited to your style and those which are not. You will find that some techniques are more natural for you than others.

Rather than waste time trying to conquer any single technique which continues to give you trouble, spend your time perfecting the techniques you prefer. You will learn more in this course than you ever need to know for practical self-defense. Thus it is much more useful to have a smaller number of defenses and do them well than it is to have a large number of defenses only partially learned.

DON'T FORGET . . .

Don't Forget is a section in each lesson to check you on the essential action in the day's work. In class work, under the supervision of the instructor, these are the points which the teacher will make most often. The section is, therefore, a repetition of instruction in the lesson which merits your special attention.

USES OF YELLING AND OTHER SOUNDS

Yelling and other sounds are physical and psychological aids in learning and in using self-defense techniques.

As a physical aid you can compare yelling to the unconscious grunt which most people make when they lift a heavy object. We commonly accompany an extreme physical effort with a sudden exhalation of breath, with or without sound. The effect of this is to tighten the muscles of the abdomen and add power to our physical action. A yell helps to release extra energy when it is most needed.

The psychological effects of yelling are well known to everyone. Yelling will scare your opponent as the whooping Indians and screaming foot soldier can testify. Not only does the yell scare your enemy, but it will confuse him and give you additional courage.

The First Day

Before beginning any practice of the exercises, read the introductory material carefully.

The techniques which you will practice on the first day are neither difficult nor complicated. Move through them slowly and gently, and do not expect to be perfect at the beginning. Be content if you get the "feel" of the actions during the first lesson.

LESSON OUTLINE

Straight-Arm Bar.
Where and how to strike.
1. The Temple Blow—Side of the Hand
2. The Bridge-of-the-Nose Blow—Side of the Hand
3. The Base-of-the-Nose Blow—Side of the Hand
Fist-Fighting Defense—Blocking the Attack
First Fall—Basic Back Fall
Hip Throw—Basic Steps (Balance Only)

Don't Forget . . .

STRAIGHT–ARM BAR

This hold is used to control and subdue an opponent who does not threaten serious attack. The technique is not practical against an opponent who is threatening a fist-fighting attack, or in any other serious situation. The specific actions of the opponent are not important, but the general situation is one in which a belligerent, possibly drunken, adversary moves forward with a reaching action, intent on pushing, pulling or grabbing you.

Remember that in a great number of attacks, your adversary must reach out for you. It is at the reaching-out point that you should apply the arm bar.

1. As your partner (right) reaches for you, use an open hand slash to strike at the nerve center of his forearm which is about 2½" below the elbow. This reduces his resistance to your next action.

2. With your right hand, grasp his right wrist and pull his arm forward.

3. Step back with your right foot into a "T" position as you turn his arm over so that his elbow is toward you. Make a fist with your left hand.

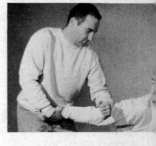

4. Keeping his captured arm pulled straight, strike sharply against his elbow with the center of your left forearm. As you strike, pull his wrist up, forcing him to his knees. Or you can push forward with your left forearm and control him.

When practicing, move slowly at first. Hit very lightly, barely touching your opponent. As you gain greater control of your own movements you may work with more speed and simulate a heavy blow, pulling it before making contact.

WHERE AND HOW TO STRIKE

Using the side of an open hand for slashing is more effective than using a fist blow. With it you may deliver a blow of considerable force without hurting your own hand, and the blow has greater penetrating power and requires less effort.

A strong, heavy person can hit out blindly with some result. As we will always assume that you are smaller than your adversary, you must make every blow count. Striking into the weak and vulnerable areas of the body is your compensation for less power. Remember—a moderate blow to any nerve center will accomplish far more than your most powerful blow struck at random.

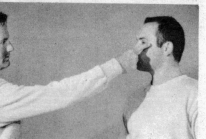 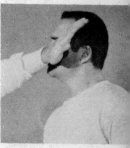

1. The Temple Blow. Strike about 1½" back from and slightly above the outer corner of the eye. A moderate blow will give pain and will stun. A heavy blow to this area can result in unconsciousness. An extremely forceful, smashing blow to the temple could be fatal and should not be used unless your life is threatened.

It requires more skill and training to deliver a fatal blow than is generally thought. Beginners lack the necessary power, accuracy and skill. When a student has gained the ability to strike such a blow, he will also have achieved the measure of control which allows him to regulate the force and effect of his striking power.

2. This blow is delivered with the fleshy part of the outside edge of the open hand, palm held downward. The thumb is held against the hand, the fingers are held together and slightly cupped. The arm from the elbow to the end of the fingers should be a straight line. When practicing, simply touch the striking area lightly. In actual use, the blow is delivered with a whipping action, letting the hand bounce back after contact.

3. The Bridge-of-the-Nose Blow. A moderate blow to the bridge of the nose is painful; a heavy blow is extremely painful.

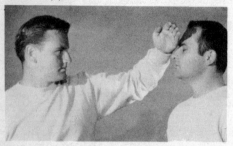

4. Striking with the fleshy part of the outside edge of the hand, hit down onto the bridge of the nose. When practicing, touch lightly and make certain that you use only the fleshy, protected area of your hand. In actual use, a smashing blow should be used.

5. The Base-of-the-Nose Blow. Striking up under the nose, contrary to wide belief, is not a dangerous blow. A moderate blow will cause considerable pain, possibly a nosebleed. A heavy blow will cause great pain, stun your opponent, and may even break the nose.

In all my experience, I have never heard of a death resulting from a broken nose. It is quite possible that a person whose nose is broken will not even lose consciousness. The principal value of this blow is the pain and confusion which result from it. Using the fleshy part of the outside edge of the palm, strike up at your opponent. In actual use, a sharp, snappy blow with follow-through will jar his head backward.

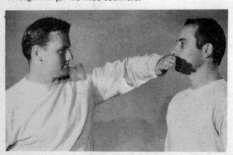

FIST-FIGHTING DEFENSE—Blocking the Attack

You will recall that we always assume your adversary is larger and heavier than you are. This also means that his arms are longer and that he should not be allowed to get within reach of your chin with his fist. To assure the success of your retaliation, you must first stop the intended attack. There are three parts involved in the complete fist-fighting defense which you will learn in this course: (1) stopping the attack, (2) retaliation, and (3) control. In this lesson, the partners will block one, then several, then many blows. In a fight, you are not expected to stand and block blows indefinitely. The practice of blocking is meant to build up the efficiency, accuracy, and speed of your response. At the start you may be able to block only one or two blows of moderate speed. As you progress, you should speed up and vary the blows until both you and your partner are quick and effective in stopping the attack.

2. The attacking partner strikes with his left fist aimed at the upper part of the defending partner's body. At the first sign of the attack, the defending partner should release the spring tension blow to block the attacker's forearm with a sharp blow, using his own forearm and blocking the blow near the attacker's wrist. The blow should be delivered in an upward and outward direction. During practice, only moderate blocking blows should be used. The attacking partner will notice that his arm feels weak after a few moments of this kind of practice, and it will be readily understood how heavy blocking blows in actual use will weaken an adversary and impair his fist-fighting ability.

1. Partners should stand facing each other. The defending partner (shown at the right) is in the preliminary fighting stance (ready stance) with his hands in the "spring tension" position. His left hand is hooked over his right hand, pulling back on it. The right hand strains forward so that tension results.

3. The attacking partner directs the same fist blow but this time with his right fist. The defender blocks the blow as before but with the left forearm.

4. The attacking partner directs a fist blow with his left fist to the lower part of the body. The defender blocks this blow by striking downward and out on the attacker's forearm near the wrist.

Practice in the order just given. The attacking partner should slowly speed up his attack as the defending partner learns to cope with it. Finally the attacking partner should mix blows and feints at varying speeds as progress is made in training.

The defending partner should avoid blocking across his body. He should keep his eyes on the attacking partner's chest in order to anticipate the direction of the next blow.

5. The attacker directs the same blow with his right fist. The defender blocks the blow in the same way as in No. 4 but uses his left forearm.

FIRST FALL—Basic Back Fall

This is the basic back fall. It is learned in preparation for more advanced falling. In the first lesson, you should try to get the feeling of rolling back gently and not thrusting or ramming yourself back. When you are timing the slap correctly, you should have no sensation of jarring your body as you fall.

1. Start from this seated position with your hands on your knees and your back slightly rounded.

3. Slap the ground with vigor just before the upper part of your back touches the ground. Your head should never touch the ground. Slapping should be done with your fingers slightly spread and your hands slightly cupped. In this way most of the shock will be absorbed by your hands. Your hands will bounce up after making contact with the ground.

2. Fall back gently, keeping your back rounded. Raise your arms, preparing to slap the ground, and keep your head forward.

HIP THROW—Basic Steps (Balance Only)

The Hip Throw is the basic body throw. It has the advantage of taking your opponent off the ground and giving you great control.

In Photo No. 1, the partners stand facing each other.

1. Partners stand facing each other in the starting position. The partner on the right is the thrower, and the partner on the left is the receiver.

2. The thrower steps diagonally across his own body with his left foot and places his left foot in front of the receiver's left foot, with his toes pointing toward the receiver. This is the beginning of the pivot.

Each partner holds the other with his right hand grasping cloth at the lapel (or lapel area) and his left hand holding the cloth at the elbow area. Study the photo for proper placement. This starting position will be used for all throws in which a normal throwing stance is indicated.

3. The thrower shifts his weight to the ball of his left foot and pivots in a counter-clockwise direction. He moves his body around and stops when he is directly in front of the receiver's body. Both the thrower's feet are now directly in front of the receiver's feet. As the pivot is executed, the thrower's right arm circles around the receiver's waist. When his feet are in correct position and his arm is around the receiver's waist, the thrower bends his knees so that his hip is on the front of the receiver's thigh and then leans the upper part of his body to the left.

4. With his arm firmly around the receiver's waist, the thrower clamps the receiver's body against his own right hip by pulling forward and slowly pulls the receiver onto his right hip by pulling forward and around with his left hand and forward with his right arm. The thrower should move his hips slightly against the receiver's thighs, thus breaking the receiver's balance and making his feet leave the ground.

DON'T FORGET

• In the Straight-Arm Bar, the essential action is keeping the arm straight and turned over so that the elbow is up. When practicing, don't strike, just press at the elbow. In actual use, strike hard.

• Touch lightly when practicing Where and How to Strike. Use the fleshy part of the edge of the hand, not the bony edge or fingers.

• Blocking is a snappy, bouncing action. Avoid trying to push at the attacking arm. Avoid hitting across the body. Use your left arm to block his right arm and your right arm to block his left arm.

• When you are practicing how to fall, your head should never touch the ground. Your hands should slap in close to your body before your upper back touches the ground. Use a gentle, rolling back motion in the fall, and avoid driving or thrusting yourself backward.

• When balancing yourself for the Hip Throw, your knees must be slightly bent and pointed outward. Your weight must be distributed equally on both feet.

The Second Day

Begin by reviewing briefly everything in the first day's lesson. You will need this review for the first few lessons in order to help you retain what you have learned. As you progress, you will find that you remember more and more easily.

LESSON OUTLINE

Review Instruction:

Straight-Arm Bar (p. 32)
Where and How to Strike
Fist-Fighting Defense—Blocking the Attack (p. 35)
First Fall (p. 37)
Hip Throw (Balance Only) (p. 38)

New Instruction:

Pushing Defense
Where and How to Strike:
  1. The Ear Nerve-Center Blow—Side of the Hand
  2. The Jaw Nerve-Center Blow—Fingertips
  3. The Side-of-the-Neck Nerve-Center Blow—Side of the Hand
Fist-Fighting Defense—Blocking the Attack and Striking Back
Second Fall—Basic Side Fall
Hip Throw—Executing the Throw and Learning to Receive

Don't Forget . . .

PUSHING DEFENSE

Use this simple defense when stronger tactics would not be appropriate. This is a situation in which your opponent is not attempting to harm or injure you but is being offensive and annoying. Frequently you will find that this type of person will back down if you speak to him in a firm and authoritative manner; if he will not be persuaded, you can use the Pushing Defense.

1. The attacking partner (shown at the right) pushes at his opponent's chest.

2. The defending partner clamps both hands over the attacking partner's hand. The clamp is applied on the back of the hand, not on the wrist or fingers. He then locks the pushing hand tight into his chest, stepping back with the right foot into the "T" position for strong balance.

3. A close-up of the hand position.

4. The defender applies pressure by bowing forward from the waist, using his chest to lever the captured fingers backward, thus forcing his opponent down. Bending the knees will make the action more effective. A snapping body motion can drive the opponent to the ground.

When practicing, the partners should do this in slow motion. Be sure to release instantly when your partner taps his submission.

WHERE AND HOW TO STRIKE

1. The Ear Nerve-Center Blow. The nerve-center area is in the little hollow under the ear lobe. The direction of the blow should be inward and up with the target point the tip of the lobe. This is a jarring, painful blow. It is not dangerous, but it can be very effective. I call this a "release" blow because after you strike, your adversary will often let go of any grip he may have on you.

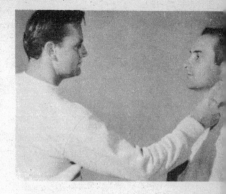

2. Deliver the blow from the side, with the edge of your hand, and your palm up.

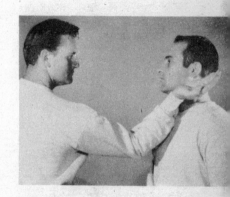

3. The Jaw Nerve-Center Blow. There is another nerve-center under the jaw, inside, not on, the jaw bone.

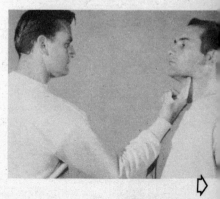

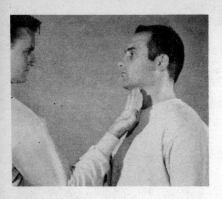

4. Strike with your fingertips, your palm toward you and your hand slightly cupped. This is a painful blow when you are very close to your adversary but not dangerous. Strike with your fingertips only when the target area is a soft part of the body.

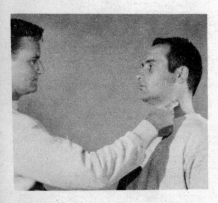

5. The Side-of-the-Neck Nerve-Center Blow. There is a heavy concentration of nerves and important veins and arteries located in the side of the neck halfway between the ear and shoulder. A moderate blow there will result in great pain and stun your adversary. A forceful blow to the side of the neck may cause unconsciousness, with very little danger of injury or lasting ill effect.

The side of the neck is an ideal target because it is an open area, not normally guarded, and also because it is exceptionally vulnerable to blows without having the danger of permanently injuring your opponent. An opponent who cannot be subdued with pain, i.e., a drunk, a wildly enraged person, even someone under the influence of a drug, can be controlled without resorting to dangerous tactics by being struck in this area.

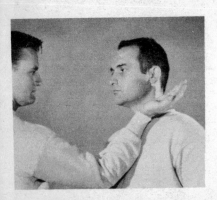

6. Deliver the blow from the side with the edge of your hand, your palm up.

FIST–FIGHTING DEFENSE—
Blocking Attack and Striking Back

This is a continuation of the Fist-Fighting Defense started in the first day's lesson.

1. The defending partner (right) blocks a single blow or a two-fist attack.

2. The defending partner counter-attacks with an open-hand blow to one of the nerve centers.

3. The defending partner follows through with a knuckle blow into the abdomen. Simulate sharp kicks into shins with edge of shoe.

SECOND FALL—Basic Side Fall

This fall and the first fall are excellent warm-up exercises, and you may do them for a minute each day or before every practice session.

The end position of this fall is also used in advanced falls to the side.

1. Starting position. Lie flat on your back, your head off the ground, your right hand in front of your face.

2. Roll gently to your right side, bringing your left leg over your right leg and preparing your right hand to slap the ground.

3. Complete the gentle roll until you are lying full on the right side, with your right leg extended and your head off the ground. The bottom of your left foot and your right hand should hit the ground simultaneously. From this position roll over gently to your left side, hitting the ground with your left hand and the bottom of your right foot. Repeat the rolling back and forth until you have the feel of the rolling and slapping action and are hitting with the proper hand and foot. Work slowly at first, gradually increasing your speed as your coordination of these actions improves.

HIP THROW—
Executing the Throw and Learning to Receive

This throw is executed with three distinct motions done simultaneously, although they are described here as separate motions. When you understand what the three motions are, you may practice them as one continuous action. Start with the position shown in Photo No. 4 (page 39).

1. (a) Straighten your knees with springy action; (b) Have both arms describe a circle, pulling to the left; (c) Make sure that the upper body turns to follow and assist the action of the arms.

2. Be sure to help your partner hit the ground gently by maintaining your grip around his waist and easing him off your hip. Practice the throws on a suitable surface, such as a lawn, beach, thick rug, or gym mat.

4. When your partner is in the proper end position, release the waist hold and step back into a strong balance position. Notice that both partners maintain the sleeve grip throughout the throw. When you have learned the proper falling techniques, the waist grip will be discarded.

3. When your partner is on the ground, continue to hold him at the waist and at the sleeve until he is in the correct ending position. Photo No. 3, Second Fall (page 46).

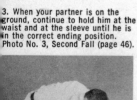

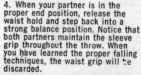

DON'T FORGET

• In the Pushing Defense, use a firm clamp on the back of the hand. Bend from the waist to get pressure on the fingers.

• In practicing Where and How to Strike, be gentle and cautious.

• In the fist-fighting strike-back practice, pull your punches.

• Second Fall: Your head should never touch the ground. Your hand and foot slap the ground at the same time. Keep your arm straight for the slap.

• Hip Throw: Don't drop or fling your partner to the ground. Let him down gently and correct his ending position before continuing.

The Third Day

From now on, your sessions should begin with the First and Second Falls for warm-up, plus any other falls that are specified for review work.

Bear in mind that you are still in the beginning stages of your training. As you begin to realize how easy these techniques are, you will be tempted to try them against stronger resistance. Don't! Be patient and you will make the best progress. You are learning—not fighting.

LESSON OUTLINE

Review Instruction:

Straight-Arm Bar (p. 32)
Pushing Defense (p. 42)
Where and How to Strike—Lessons for First and Second Days
Fist-Fighting Defense—Blocking the Attack and Striking Back (p. 45)
Falls No. 1 and 2 (p. 37, 46)
Hip Throw—Throwing and Receiving (p. 47)

New Instruction:

Back-Choke Defense—Finger Grip
Where and How to Strike:
  1. The Neck Nerve-Center Blow—Extended Knuckle
  2. The Windpipe or Adam's Apple Blow—Y of the Hand
  3. The Throat-Hollow Blow—Fingertips
Fist-Fighting Defense—Block and Throw
Third Fall—Basic Side Roll
Swinging-Leg Throw—Basic Steps (Position Only)

Don't Forget . . .

BACK–CHOKE DEFENSE—Finger Grip

The great virtue of this defense is its simplicity. Even a child would find it an effective defense against an adult's attack.

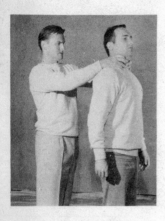

1. In a surprise attack from the rear, your opponent grips your throat with his fingers, digging into your windpipe.

2. As the defender, you should grip both of the attacker's little fingers. It is best to grip the little fingers, because they are ordinarily not used for choking and so are easier to grab, and the pain caused by the action is just as effective against the little fingers as against any other. It is possible to use this defense by gripping any other finger, however.

3. Pull sharply on either of the captured fingers, bending it backward. When practicing you should do this very slowly. In actual use, if the action is quick and sharp enough, it is possible to dislocate the finger. As you jerk the finger, turn to prepare yourself to kick the attacker.

4. Maintaining your grip on the captured finger, kick sharply into the attacker's shin with the bottom of your shoe.
When practicing, pull your kick and touch your partner slightly. In actual use, you should continue to kick until your adversary is subdued.

WHERE AND HOW TO STRIKE

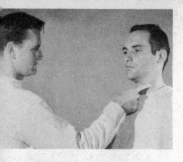

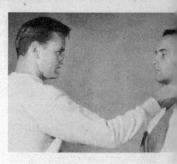

1. The Neck Nerve-Center Blow. There is a vertical neck muscle on either side of the windpipe. The nerve is located in the center of this muscle. A light blow to it will cause pain and result in soreness. The blow should be directed at a 45° angle.

2. When you strike, the center knuckle should be extended. An extended knuckle blow should be used only into soft areas of the body. A digging motion will produce moderate pain; a jabbing blow, extreme pain.

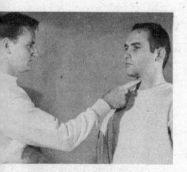

3. The Windpipe, or Adam's Apple Blow. Avoid striking the windpipe unless your life is threatened. A heavy blow there can be fatal. A light blow or squeezing action will subdue an adversary who is otherwise insensitive to pain.

4. Use the "Y" of the open hand for this blow. This is not as dangerous as a side-of-the-hand blow or fist, because the pressure is spread over a wider area.

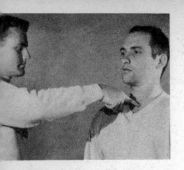 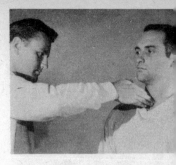

5. The Throat-Hollow Blow. This, too, is a dangerous blow, and you should not use it unless your life is threatened.

6. The blow is made by pushing the fingertips into the hollow at the base of the neck. A light, digging motion will result in considerable pain. Avoid a heavy blow.
   Note: Use only the effort required to stop and subdue your opponent. There is no necessity or justification for violent and dangerous techniques unless your life is threatened.

FIST–FIGHTING DEFENSE—Block and Throw

After blocking and retaliating with hand and foot blows, complete the defensive action in a fist fight by subduing your adversary with a throw.

Quite possibly you will have stopped the fist-fighting attack when you have blocked your opponent's blows (see the first day's lesson). Sometimes the fight continues to the stage of striking and kicking (see the second day's lesson). Less often you will be forced to finish the fight with a throw. Putting your adversary on the ground is both a physical and a psychological victory. You should learn the full action as if it were necessary in every case so that you can carry through to the end if necessary.

The situation will determine how your adversary is to be thrown. If you are mainly concerned with a psychological victory, you may lower him to the ground, supporting part of his weight as he goes over. If you are dealing with a more serious attack, you may either throw your adversary with ordinary force or dash him heavily to the ground.

Note: Never attempt a throw without using the weakening techniques first. Unless you take the fight out of your adversary, it is very difficult and impractical to try to throw him. Only a person with many years of training in Judo could move quickly enough for a throw against an experienced street fighter. In the movies the villains go flying over the heroes' shoulders because they are paid to do so, but you had better be more careful and less showy.

1. You have already stopped your adversary's attack with blocking and have kicked and struck in retaliation. When your opponent is obviously weakened by these actions, but not yet subdued, you can continue. Grip his sleeves or his arm if he is not wearing a shirt or jacket.

2. Spread and lock your opponent's arms out and begin to break his balance by turning his body. As you do this, place your left foot in front of his left foot, with your toes pointing to the left as you prepare for the pivot.

3. Pivot on the ball of your left foot, and place your right foot in front of his right foot while sliding your arm around his waist as you turn.
   Your feet should now be directly in front of his feet. Your knees should be bent so that your

hip is against his thigh. Now bend to the left with the upper part of your body.

4. With both arms, pull your opponent onto your hip, as described in the Hip Throw.

THIRD FALL—Basic Side Roll

Whether or not you intend to go on into Sport Judo, you should practice this fall. As a safety fall it is superior to other types of rolling falls. If you intend to practice throwing with your partner, you will need this fall so that you may receive the throws safely and without discomfort.

1. Starting position. Place your feet shoulder-width apart, with your toes pointing slightly outward. Your right hand should be placed on the ground directly in front of you, forming a triangle with your feet. Your weight should be distributed equally on both feet and the right hand. Place your left hand in the center of the triangle with your left elbow pointing out at a 45° angle. Both your arms should be bent slightly, but held firm.

2. Start your roll by shifting your weight onto your right hand and left foot. Raise your right foot.

3. Tuck your head in so that it does not touch the ground as you roll over. Now roll gently over your left forearm, upper arm, and shoulder.

5. Continue the action until you finish on your right side, slapping with your right hand and left foot. This is the ending described in the second fall.

4. Continue the roll slowly across your back.

SWINGING–LEG THROW—Basic Steps (Position Only)

1. The partners assume the basic starting position for the throw. The partner shown at the right is the thrower.

2. The thrower steps forward with his left foot, placing it beside the receiver's right foot. As the thrower takes this step, he should twist the receiver's body back and around, thus weakening his balance.

3. With the receiver now badly balanced, the thrower starts the throw by swinging his right leg up.

4. The thrower brings his right leg down in back of the receiver's right leg at the calf, lifting it slightly off the ground. Simultaneously the thrower moves his arms and upper body down and around to keep the receiver in motion and off balance.

This is a fine throw for use in self-defense. A small person can manage it easily, without having to carry his opponent's weight.

DON'T FORGET

- When practicing the Back-Choke Defense, use an easy motion. In a fight, jerk the finger back sharply.
- Where and How to Strike. No injury to the extended knuckle is possible when striking into soft parts of the body.
- Do not use any blow to the windpipe unless your life is threatened.
- It is easy and tempting to throw hard once you have your partner in position. Don't. Remember it will be his turn to practice throwing next.
- Third Fall: Don't let your head touch the ground at any time in this fall. Keep your left arm firm and bent; don't let it buckle or you will bang your shoulder. Slap the mat hard with your hand and foot. Stay in position and let your partner check to see that you have finished correctly.
- Swinging-Leg Throw: Break your opponent's balance before swinging your leg. Follow through with the swinging leg, hitting calf-to-calf.

The Fourth Day

In review work, although you are not to expect speedy performance of the defenses, you should practice complete actions without hesitations between steps. If you are going too fast, your technique will be sloppy. If this happens, slow down to a pace that allows you to do the exercise smoothly.

LESSON OUTLINE

Review Instruction:

Falls No. 1, 2, 3
Straight-Arm Bar (p. 32)
Pushing Defense (p. 42)
Back-Choke Defense——Finger Grip (p. 50)
Where and How to Strike——Lessons for First through Third Day
Fist-Fighting Defense——Block and Throw (p. 53)
Hip Throw——Throwing and Receiving (p. 47)
Swinging-Leg Throw——(Position Only) (p. 55)

New Instruction:

Wrist-Grab Defense——One-Hand Grip
Where and How to Strike:
1. The Base-of-the-Neck Blow——Side of the Hand
2. The Inside-Joint-of-the-Elbow Blow——Side of the Hand
3. The Forearm-Nerve Blow——Side of the Hand
Fist-Fighting Defense——Double Kick, Block, Retaliation, and Throw
Swinging-Leg Throw——Completion of Throw and Receiving

Don't Forget . . .

WRIST–GRAB DEFENSE—One-Hand Grip

Having your wrist grabbed is not in itself a serious attack, but you must learn to escape quickly to avoid further aggressive action.

1. The attacking partner, shown at the left, grabs the wrist of the defending partner.

2. The defender should place his free hand, palm down, on the attacker's grabbing wrist.

3. Maintaining this placement of his free hand, the defender should jerk his captured hand in and up to effect its release. The movement in and up works against the thumb and forefinger, the weakest part of the attacker's grip. In order to learn this properly, the defender should do this in slow motion, without resistance from his partner.

4. The defender now jerks his freed hand across his body, pushing against his opponent's wrist to keep it down.

5. If necessary, the defender may finish the defense with a cross-body, edge-of-the-hand blow to the nerve centers in the head or neck.

WHERE AND HOW TO STRIKE

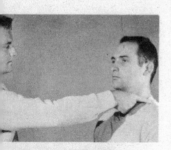

1. The Base-of-the-Neck Blow. Strike the neck where the shoulder and neck join. A moderate blow is painful; a forceful blow can numb the entire arm. This is not a dangerous area to strike, and yet a moderate blow can be very effective.

2. Deliver the blow with an open hand, the edge of your hand, palm turned in. A vertical, chopping action is best.

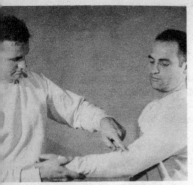

3. The Inside-Joint-of-the-Elbow Blow. Striking here has a double effect. This is a nerve center and therefore pain will result, and a sharp blow will bend the arm.

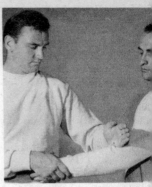

4. Slash downward with the side of the hand.

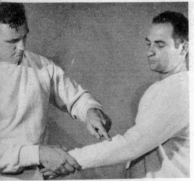

5. The Forearm-Nerve Blow. The nerve is about 2½" down from the elbow. If you extend your arm, you will find the nerve center just below the crest of the mound of the muscle. A heavy blow there can numb or temporarily paralyze the forearm and hand.

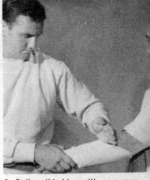

6. Deliver this blow with your open hand, using a sharp and snappy movement.

FIST–FIGHTING DEFENSE—Double Kick, Block, Retaliation, and Throw

I consider this combination to be the most effective and versatile defense against a number of serious, frontal attacks.

It does not matter what specific type of attack is being used (the sole exception is weapons, and they are taken up later in this course), and you do not have to lose precious time determining the attacker's specific intent. Assume that someone is coming at you with obviously aggressive intentions. Your defense should begin before he has approached close enough to hit you with his fists, or to grab or touch you. Your defense will always be more effective if you start it before you are in range of a fist blow.

1. When your attacker gets within kicking range, but before he is in fist-fighting range, turn your body to the side, and kick with the bottom of your shoe into his knee.

When practicing, be careful to pull your kick. Approximately 65 pounds of pressure is sufficient to dislocate the knee and you have much greater force when you use your full kicking power.

2. Place your kicking leg behind you, and turn to kick with your other foot into the shin.

Note: At any point in this combination defense, you may find that your adversary is ready to stop his attack. When he is subdued, you must not continue the retaliation. However, you should learn the full defense, so that you have the ability to carry through. ⇨

3. Assume that your adversary will try to deliver fist blows, and block both of his arms.

4. Continue your defense delivering hand and foot blows simultaneously. Not only will they hurt your opponent but they will confuse his attack by making him unable to guard all the places that are being hit at the same time.

5. By now your adversary should be considerably weakened. You can finish the defense with a hip throw.

1. Execute this throw by a vigorous swinging-leg action, hitting the receiver with your calf to his calf. Follow through with your kick to lift his kicked leg high. Continuous twist-and-turn arm movement is essential for a successful throw.

2. During practice, maintain your grip on the receiver's lapel and sleeve to ease his fall.

3. When the receiver is able to fall properly, the thrower should release the lapel grip as the throw is executed.

DON'T FORGET

· Wrist-Grab Defense: Be sure to withdraw your hand *across* your body in order to protect your face and be ready to strike back.

· Where and How to Strike: To find exactly the right spot dig into the area with your thumb until your partner feels some sensation of pain.

The Fifth Day

It is better to do all the review work quickly rather than to attempt to perfect any single technique. You are still in the beginning stages of your study, and you should not demand too much of yourself.

LESSON OUTLINE

Review Instruction:

Falls No. 1, 2, 3
Straight-Arm Bar (p. 32)
Pushing Defense (p. 42)
Back-Choke Defense—Finger Grip (p. 50)
Wrist-Grab Defense—One-Hand Grip (p. 58)
Where and How to Strike—Lessons for First through
   Fourth Days
Fist-Fighting Defense—Fourth-Day Work
Swinging-Leg Throw—Throwing and Receiving (p. 63)

New Instruction:

Wrist Hold No. 1
Wrist-Grab Defense—One-Hand Grip across Body
Where and How to Strike:
   1. The Wrist Blow—Forearm
   2. The Back-of-the-Hand Blow—Extended Knuckle
   3. The Side-of-the-Body Blow—Side of the Fist
Fourth Fall—Standing Fall Back
Bent-Arm Hip Throw—Basic Steps (Balance Only)

Don't Forget . . .

Wrist Hold No. 1

Many attacks begin with a reaching gesture. If you learn to cope with the reaching arm before your adversary has touched you, you will then be dealing with an easier situation. It does not matter if your opponent intends to grab, poke, pull, or slap—he must reach out to start his attack.

Note: This is an effective defense against an annoying or insulting opponent, one who does not threaten serious harm. Do not attempt holding techniques when the attacker is violent.

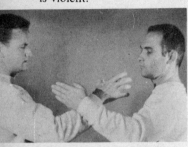

1. The attacking partner, left, reaches for the defender. The defending partner strikes at the forearm nerve center with a side-of-the-hand blow, thus distracting and weakening the attacker.

2. The defender should then grip the attacker's hand, placing his thumb on the back of the hand, his fingers into the palm.

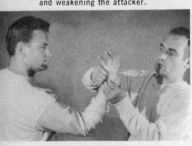

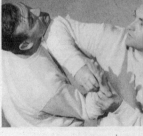

3. The defender takes the same grip with his right hand. He is now holding the attacker's hand with a natural grip.

4. The defender should place his right elbow into his opponent's neck, simultaneously taking a step with his right foot that places him at his opponent's right side. Pressure is applied by locking the secured hand into the defender's chest, pushing into the attacker's neck and twisting his secured hand in a counter-clockwise direction. The defender can finish the defense by executing the Swinging-Leg Throw.

WRIST–GRAB DEFENSE—One-Hand Grip across Body

1. The attacking partner, shown left, grips your wrist with one hand, across your body. First make a fist of your captured hand.

2. Then, with your free hand, reach over your partner's arm and grip your own captured fist. Jerk down.

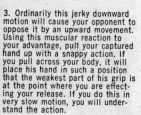

3. Ordinarily this jerky downward motion will cause your opponent to oppose it by an upward movement. Using this muscular reaction to your advantage, pull your captured hand up with a snappy action. If you pull across your body, it will place his hand in such a position that the weakest part of his grip is at the point where you are effecting your release. If you do this in very slow motion, you will understand the action.

4. In addition to giving you an easy release, the cross-body action puts your hand in position for a quick counterblow, if necessary, and places you in a strong defensive position.

5. You may continue with simultaneous hand blows to subdue your opponent.

WHERE AND HOW TO STRIKE

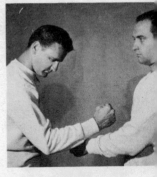

1. The Wrist Blow. A moderate blow can cause numbing; a heavy blow can immobilize the hand temporarily.

2. Strike with the center of the forearm at the wrist. It does not require great accuracy to make use of this blow.

3. **The Back-of-the-Hand Blow.**
Strike into the back of the
hand using an extended center
knuckle. This is a painful blow
and is excellent for effecting
release if the opponent is
gripping or grabbing.

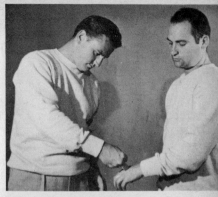

4. **The Side-of-the-Body Blow.**
Strike in an upward direction
under the last rib. You can find
the proper spot by poking
yourself or your partner with
your finger.

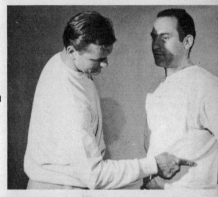

5. For this blow use the side
of your fist. The blow may also
be struck using the side-of-the-
hand slash or the extended
knuckle.

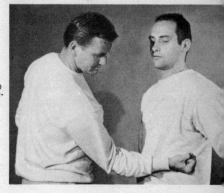

FOURTH FALL—Standing Fall Back

This is an advanced form of the First Fall. It is useful if you are pushed, thrown, or trip backward.

1. Step back with your left foot and extend your arms to maintain balance.

2. Lean forward as though you were about to touch your toes.

3. Sit as close to your heel and as close to the ground as possible. Raise your arms to prepare to slap the mat. Curl your back.

4. Fall back gently—do not thrust or drive yourself back—slapping the mat at a 45° angle to your body as your belt touches it. Be sure that your head does not touch the mat.

BENT–ARM HIP THROW—Basic Steps (Balance Only)

The Bent-Arm Hip Throw is a variation of the basic Hip Throw. It allows you to throw an adversary whom you have already gripped without changing your hand position. To the beginner it will seem much more awkward than the basic throw, but its advantages will be noted as training progresses.

1. Partners face each other in a natural stance and prepare to execute the throw. The partner at the right is the thrower.

2. The thrower places his left foot in front of the receiver's left foot and starts to pivot.

3. Without releasing his right-hand grip on the receiver's lapel, the thrower completes his pivot, places his right elbow under the receiver's right armpit and bends his knees.

4. The thrower pulls the receiver onto his hip by straightening his knees slightly as he pulls down and around with his left hand while the bent right arm pulls up and forward.

DON'T FORGET

• Wrist Hold No. 1: Be sure your thumbs are side-by-side at the back of your opponent's hand. Pressure should be mainly from your body motion, rather than from your fingers.

• Wrist-Grab Defense: Pull across your body with a jerky, snappy motion. If your adversary is very strong, a kick into his shin will aid in effecting the release.

• Where and How to Strike: Remember to practice all blows first with one hand and then the other.

• Bent-Arm Hip Throw: Lock your elbow firmly into your partner's armpit. In a properly balanced position you should easily support your partner's weight. When the upper part of your body leans to the left, your partner should be on your *hip*.

First Progress Test

This is a test of the general knowledge you have acquired up to this point in the training. After you have marked your answers, check them with the correct answers on page 224. For each question there is only one proper answer.

1. Of the Basic Stances, the best stance for a strong position for defense or attack is:
   A. Natural Stance.
   B. "T" Position.
   C. One-Point Balance.
2. A fighting stance puts you into strong balance and gives you protection from attack. A fighting stance shows your adversary that:
   A. You are a tough guy and an expert.
   B. You are confused and are trying to trick him.
   C. You are obviously prepared for action.
3. The natural grip can best be compared to:
   A. Shaking hands.
   B. Pushing a doorbell.
   C. Thumbing a ride.
4. An unnatural grip can best be described as:
   A. The opposite of the natural grip.
   B. The natural grip turned backwards.
   C. The opposite of pushing a doorbell.
5. Striking and kicking at a suspended ball is training for:
   A. Power and accuracy.
   B. Coordination and accuracy.
   C. Power and exercise.
6. Striking and kicking at a heavy bag is training for:
   A. Power and accuracy.
   B. Coordination and accuracy.
   C. Power and exercise.

7. Safety in practice requires:
    A. Moderate pressure and tapping for submission.
    B. Smooth, slow action and pulling your blows and kicks.
    C. Everything in A and B.
8. The straight-arm-bar technique calls for pressure to be applied:
    A. Down at the elbow.
    B. Up at the elbow.
    C. From the side.
9. The side-of-the-neck blow should be:
    A. Delivered with a high kick.
    B. Relied on because the neck is an ideal target with little danger of injury.
    C. Avoided because of the great possibility of injury.
10. In executing the Swinging-Leg Throw you must kick back, hitting calf-to-calf. The kick must be executed:
    A. After the opponent's balance is broken.
    B. Before his balance is broken.
    C. In order to break his balance.

The Sixth Day

In your review work you should now begin to determine which techniques suit you best and which you seem to do with the greatest ease and confidence. While you build on the techniques which you like best, *continue* to review the techniques which are not as appealing.

LESSON OUTLINE

Review Instruction:

Falls No. 1 through 4
Back-Choke Defense—Finger Grip (p. 50)
Wrist Hold No. 1 (p. 66)
Wrist-Grab Defense
   One-Hand Grip (p. 58)
   One-Hand Grip across Body (p. 67)
Where and How to Strike—Lessons for Second through
   Fifth Days
Fist-Fighting Defense—Fourth-Day Work
Bent-Arm Hip Throw—(Balance Only) (p. 71)

New Instruction:

Wrist Hold No. 2
Wrist-Grab Defense—Two Hands Gripping Both Wrists
Where and How to Strike:
   1. The Solar Plexus Blow—Fist
   2. The Jaw or Face Blow—Elbow Back and Elbow
      Vertical
   3. The Abdomen Blow—Extended Knuckle
Fist-Fighting Defense—Double Kick, Block, Retaliation,
   and Swinging-Leg Throw
Bent-Arm Hip Throw—Completion of Throw and Receiving

Don't Forget . . .

WRIST HOLD NO. 2

The use of this wrist hold is the same as for the first wrist hold (page 66). Do not attempt to use it as a defense against a serious attack.

1. Your opponent, shown at the left, reaches out with an unnatural grip as if to grab and twist. You should slash at his elbow to weaken and distract him.

2. With your slashing hand grip his hand with an unnatural grip.

3. As you raise his hand, apply an unnatural grip with your other hand.

4. Raise his captured hand over his head and apply pressure by bending his wrist back and turning it clockwise. As you apply wrist pressure, step forward, which will put your opponent into a weak, off-balance position.

WRIST–GRAB DEFENSE—Two Hands Gripping Both Wrists

To repeat, having your wrist or wrists grabbed in this fashion is not particularly dangerous, but you will be partially immobilized and must learn to effect a quick release.

1. Your opponent, shown at the left, grips both your wrists, with a natural grip.

2. Using a snappy, jerking action, swing both your arms outward four to six inches. Your opponent's natural reaction will be to resist your outward thrust by pushing inward.

3. Using the force of his inward push, jerk your hands in and up against his thumbs, the weakest part of his grip.

4. Pull your arms up and out at a 45° angle.

5. If necessary, you may retaliate by striking down across his arms while delivering a high blow with your other hand.

WHERE AND HOW TO STRIKE

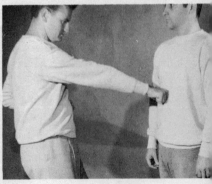

1. The Solar Plexus Blow. Strike into the solar plexus, where the ribs part. A straight blow will cause moderate pain and can knock the wind out of your opponent or make him nauseated. Striking upward with force will affect the heart, liver, and lungs. A heavy blow directed upward should be used only in case of violent attack as it may cause serious injury and can even be fatal.

2. For a straight blow, strike with your fist into the solar plexus.

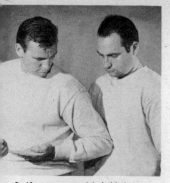

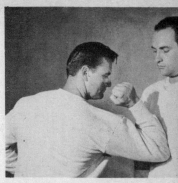

3. If your opponent is behind you, you may strike straight into his solar plexus with your elbow, keeping the palm up for greatest effectiveness. To deliver an upward elbow blow into the solar plexus from this position, drop your hand and drive your elbow upward and back.

4. A front elbow blow to the solar plexus can be made straight, as shown, or upward, by use of a swinging-elbow blow.

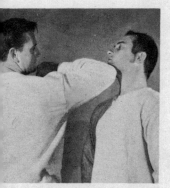

5. The Jaw or Face Blow. A horizontal blow with the elbow into the jaw (or face) is done with a circular motion.

6. The Abdomen Blow. You can strike into the abdomen (about two inches below the belt), using an extended knuckle blow. A moderate blow can be very painful, and a heavy blow can cause internal injuries.

FIST–FIGHTING DEFENSE—Double Kick, Block, Retaliation, and Swinging-Leg Throw

This is a complete defense against a fist-fighting attack and differs from the previous fist-fighting defense only by finishing with the Swinging-Leg Throw. As this particular combination of techniques is essential for a good street-fighting defense, you cannot practice it too much. The finishing throw, if necessary, is the least important part of the defense. If you ever need to use this defense in a fight, you will find that the first kicks and blows will stop almost all attacks. The throw is taught to give you additional security.

1. The man on the right assumes a fighting stance.

2. Before your adversary gets within fist-striking range, kick into his knee or thigh and continue kicking until he is weakened.

3. When your adversary is obviously hurt, deliver a kick into his shins and block both his arms simultaneously.

4. & 5. Now apply the Swinging-Leg Throw. Start by weakening your adversary's balance, using a palm-of-the-hand blow up under his jaw or Y-of-the-hand blow into his throat (p. 51), as shown in Photo No. 5.

1. This throw is executed by a simultaneous use of several moves. Though described separately, they should be done as one. (a) Spring up onto the balls of your feet. (b) Pull your opponent down and around with your left hand and forward with the bent arm. (c) Your body should move around to follow and assist the arm action.

2. As a beginner, you should maintain your grip with both hands to ease the fall of the receiver. Then step back with your right foot into a strong balance position.

DON'T FORGET

• Wrist Lock No. 2: Pressure must be applied by the double action of bending and twisting. A few kicks into the shin will assist you to control a resisting opponent.

• Wrist-Grab Defense: Faking a kick can be useful here. You may need to use the muscle reaction twice to confuse him sufficiently.

• Where and How to Strike: When practicing with your partner, simulate the blows and touch lightly at the proper place in the proper way. Practice all the blows against the bag, working to develop a snappy blow. Instead of thudding into the bag, deliver your blows so that they bounce back. Your aim is to develop speed, form, and accuracy rather than brute force.

The Seventh Day

In the review work, you should now introduce the element of surprise. Previously, you and your partner have defended and attacked with prearranged techniques. When practicing surprise attacks, you will soon discover your weak spots and be able to give them greater attention.

LESSON OUTLINE

Review Instruction:

Falls No. 1 through 4
Wrist Holds No. 1 and 2 (p. 66, 76)
Wrist-Grab Defense:
    One-Hand Grip (p. 58)
    One-Hand Grip across Body (p. 67)
    Two Hands Gripping Both Wrists (p. 77)
Where and How to Strike—Lessons for Third through
    Sixth Days
Fist-Fighting Defense:
    Hip-Throw Ending (p. 53)
    Swinging-Leg-Throw Ending (p. 80)
Bent-Arm Hip Throw—Throwing and Receiving (p. 82)

New Instruction:

Reverse Arm Lock
Wrist-Grab Defense—Two Hands Gripping One Wrist
Where and How to Strike:
    1. The Base-of-the-Skull Blow—Heel of the Palm
    2. The 7th-Vertebra Blow—Side of the Hand
    3. The Backbone Blow—Side of the Fist
Fifth Fall—Forward Roll and Staying Down
Neck-Lock Hip Throw—Basic Steps (Balance Only)

Don't Forget . . .

REVERSE ARM LOCK

You can counter a high, reaching attack very well using this arm lock. As with all locks, it is not advisable to use it in a real fight, but it is of value against a taller adversary attempting to annoy or bully you.

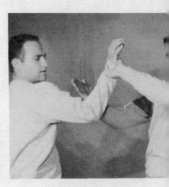

1. The attacking partner shown at the left, makes a high, grabbing motion. The defending partner slashes up at the reaching arm and steps in with his left foot at the same time.

2. The defending partner grips the attacker's wrist with his left hand, using the unnatural grip, and slashes into the attacker's elbow with his right hand with enough force to bend the arm.

3. With his right hand, the defender reaches under attacker's right arm and grips his own left hand. He can then apply pressure by pushing the attacker's arm back and down as he bows forward from the waist. If the attacker still offers resistance, the defender can kick into his shin with his right foot or step in with his right foot, placing it back of the attacker's foot, and thus put the attacker in a very awkward off-balance position. Now the defender can easily apply the Swinging-Leg Throw, or simply force the attacker to the ground.

WRIST–GRAB DEFENSE—Two Hands Gripping One Wrist

1. The attacking partner, shown at the left, grabs one wrist of the defending partner, using both hands.

2. The defending partner makes a fist of the captured hand and jerks down. This will create a muscle reaction, and the attacking partner will push up.

3. & 4. Using the force of this push up, the defender jerks up and across his body, breaking the grip. By pulling across the body, the defender is working against the weakest part of the attacker's grip —the thumbs—and ends in a good defensive position. Photo No. 4.

5. If necessary, the defender can retaliate with hand and foot blows.

WHERE AND HOW TO STRIKE

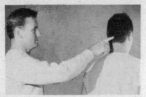

1. The Base-of-the-Skull Blow. A moderate blow will immobilize your adversary. Avoid a very heavy blow except in defense of your life, for it is possible to cause serious injury using your full power. The effect is the same as in whip-lash.

4. Any of the downward blows can be used against this area. A side-of-the-hand blow, as shown, or the side-of-the-fist or elbow blow will be effective.

2. Strike upward with the heel of the palm. This type of blow is also very effective for striking up under the chin.

5. The Backbone Blow. Strike between the shoulder blades. A powerful blow to this area can jar the heart, causing extreme pain or unconsciousness. A moderate blow will be painful.

3. The 7th-Vertebra Blow. Strike at the 7th vertebra which is weakly supported. It is possible to dislodge the bone by using a heavy blow. This is a serious injury, and a heavy blow should be used only in defense of your life. A moderate blow to this area will immobilize your adversary.

6. This blow can also be delivered with the side of the fist or with the elbow.

FIFTH FALL—Forward Roll and Staying Down

This fall is useful when you are thrust forward and cannot roll over and up to a standing position. It gives protection against an injury to your head or the base of your spine.

1. Place your feet shoulder-width apart; place your hands about 18 inches in front of your feet, pointing your fingers out to the side.

2. Tuck your head in and shift your weight from your feet to your hands. Slowly continue shifting your weight until you roll over. Your head should be kept tucked in, and your shoulders should touch the ground before the rest of your body. Do not thrust or drive yourself over; the motion should be a gentle and smooth roll.

3. The full bottom of your feet should hit the ground, with your hands out at a 45° angle. Your hands and feet should slap at the same time. Do not let your hip or head touch the ground throughout the fall. If you find that you are not finishing the fall properly, first assume the correct ending position so that you get the "feel" of how you should be ending.

NECK–LOCK HIP THROW—Basic Steps (Balance Only)

This throw is particularly effective against a tall opponent. The partners start by facing each other in a natural stance.

1. The thrower (at the right) steps across his body, places his left foot in front of the receiver's left foot (as in the Hip Throw), and begins his pivot. His right arm should be in position to slip around the receiver's neck.

2. The thrower completes the pivot, his arm around the receiver's neck.

3. The thrower bends his knees so that his hip is below the receiver's thigh, and leans the upper part of his body to the left.

4. The thrower pulls the receiver onto his hip by straightening his legs and pulling forward with his right arm while his left arm pulls around and down.

DON'T FORGET

• Reverse Arm Lock: Keep your opponent's arm bent; do not allow it to straighten. Apply the pressure back and down.
• Fifth Fall: Don't let your head touch the ground. Use a gentle roll, not a thrust to get over. Your knees should be bent at the end of the fall.
• Neck-Lock Hip Throw: The action of the right arm is pulling over and down. The left arm pulls around and down. Get your hip down to your partner's thighs for an easy lift to throwing position.

The Eighth Day

For the most effective use of hand blows versatility is essential. You should practice every type of blow you have learned against the various nerve centers. Only by trying the blows against all the areas, and alternating your right and left hands, will you be able to determine the most practical type of blow for your actual use. As with the various types of technique shown in the course, you will soon find that you have favorite blows. Without neglecting the blows you find less easy to do, stress the practice of your best blows so that you gain a strong repertoire of effective ways of striking.

LESSON OUTLINE

Review Instruction:

Falls No. 1 through 5
Wrist Holds No. 1 and 2 (p. 66, 76)
Reverse Arm Lock (p. 84)
Wrist-Grab Defenses:
    One-Hand Grip (p. 58)
    One-Hand Grip across Body (p. 67)
    Two Hands Gripping Both Wrists (p. 77)
    Two Hands Gripping One Wrist (p. 85)
Where and How to Strike—Lessons for Fourth through
    Seventh Days
Fist-Fighting Defense:
    Hip-Throw Ending (p. 53)
    Swinging-Leg-Throw Ending (p. 80)
Bent-Arm Hip Throw—Throwing and Receiving (p. 82)
Neck-Lock Hip Throw—(Balance Only) (p. 88)

New Instruction:

Grab Defense—Thumb Release
Where and How to Strike:
    1. The Kidney Blow—Extended Knuckle
    2. The Back-of-the-Upper-Leg Blow—Inside Edge of
       the Foot
    3. The Back-of-the-Knee Blow—Outside Edge of the
       Foot
Fist-Fighting Defense—Long-Range Fist Attack
Neck-Lock Hip Throw—Executing the Throw and
    Receiving

Don't Forget . . .

GRAB DEFENSE—Thumb Release

It is a good idea to learn defenses that are practical against a group of attacks. Learning a specific defense for each specific attack is highly impractical because there are literally thousands of different ways of attacking. It is much better to learn a small number of defenses which will be useful in many situations. There are, however, some situations which are so common as to be best countered by a special defense. The following is just such a situation.

1. The attacking partner, shown at the right, grabs the defending partner's lapel with a natural grip.

2. The defender draws his body back and grips the grabbing wrist with his left hand, using the unnatural grip.

3. The defender pulls back to keep the attacker's arm extended, places the heel of the palm of his right hand over the attacker's bent thumb and squeezes. The pressure should be applied mainly against the thumbnail.

4. This is the action of forcing the thumb shown in the close-up. This hold should be practiced very slowly. When it is done improperly, there is little result; when it is done properly, it will cause a great deal of pain and care must be taken not to injure the attacking partner during practice.

5. The pain that this technique will cause should be sufficient to prevent further action on the attacker's part. When his grab is released, he should be pushed away with both hands.

WHERE AND HOW TO STRIKE

1. The Kidney Blow. The kidneys are about 2 inches above the belt line and about 2 inches to each side of the backbone. A blow directed upward just under the last rib will reach the kidney area. A moderate blow to a kidney will take much of the fight out of your adversary and a heavy blow can cause serious internal injury. You should use such a blow only if your life is in danger.

2. Strike with your extended knuckle, keeping your palm up. Make a fist and extend the center knuckle. By using an extended knuckle, you concentrate the power of the blow in a small area, thus giving it additional force.

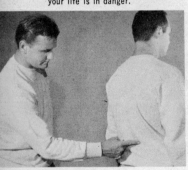

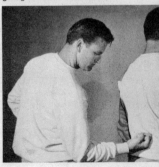

3. The Back-of-the-Upper-Leg Blow. Strike into the muscle in this area. It is better to use a kick rather than to attempt a hand blow. You can kick with force into this spot without danger of serious injury to your adversary. The result may be a muscle spasm (Charley horse) which can incapacitate the leg for a few hours and up to several days.

4. Kick with the inside edge of your shoe. The hard leather edge will add considerable power to your kick.

5. The Back-of-the-Knee Blow. A kick into the back of the knee can cause knee sprain. The purpose of this kick is to break your adversary's balance, and it may even put him on the ground.

6. The blow may also be delivered with the outside edge of the shoe. Its effect is the same as with the inside edge.

FIST-FIGHTING DEFENSE—Long-Range Fist Attack

When you are threatened by a fist fighter from a distance beyond his arm reach, you should react with your strongest defense—kicking. You may take a fighting stance and try to reason with your adversary. It is not at all unlikely that he will be dissuaded by your obvious readiness to fight in a style to which he is unaccustomed. However, do not waste time trying to reason with an opponent who is intent on attacking.

1. Your adversary threatens a fist attack but is too far from you to hit unless he takes at least one step. At the first sign of threat, assume a fighting stance.

2. As your adversary approaches, jump to the side. Push off with your right foot, and, making a big leap, land on your left foot. Leap to the outside of his striking arm. This will place you out of reach.

3. As soon as you land on your left foot, your right foot should kick into your opponent with a hooking kick. Strike with the bottom of your foot or with your toe. Lean your body well away from the opponent so that you are completely out of his fist range.

4. After kicking, there will normally be a recoil action. Place your kicking foot on the ground immediately, then turn and prepare for a second kick.

5. Your second kick should be delivered into the lower part of your adversary's body, preferably the knee.

6. & 7. This kicking action should completely subdue your opponent. However, if necessary, you should be able to continue by applying the Straight-Arm Bar, which you have already learned.

NECK–LOCK HIP THROW—Executing the Throw and Receiving

1. The throw is executed by performing several actions **simultaneously.** All of them are required for a successful throw. They are described here as separate actions so that you can easily understand them: (a) The thrower springs up onto the balls of his feet; (b) his right forearm pushes forward sharply as his left hand pulls around to the left; and (c) his body turns to assist and follow the arm action.

2. The receiver ends in Fall No. 2. Both men maintain sleeve grips. The thrower holds firmly with his left hand and pulls up to ease the fall of the receiver. The receiver maintains a sleeve grip with his right hand, also easing his fall. The partner who receives the throw should stay in the ending position until the thrower checks and corrects the ending position.

DON'T FORGET

• Grab Defense—Thumb Release: If there is space, take a full step back to pull your opponent off balance. When applying pressure, use the entire hand for the squeezing action.

• Where and How to Strike: In practice, do not strike at the kidneys. A pressing action is sufficient for training purposes.

• Long-Range Fist Attack: Kick before your adversary is within arm's reach. By looking at his chest you can determine which hand he will use for the attack and when he will move as the first indication of movement and the direction are first apparent in the chest area. Try to move to the side of your opponent when threatened by a fist attack. Two kicks are generally sufficient to discourage an adversary, but be prepared for as many as are needed. Do not rush in for the arm lock until your opponent is obviously weakened.

• Neck-Lock Hip Throw: Do not fling your partner down in practicing this throw. You cannot offer him any support and must therefore be especially careful to observe the safety rules. You should have a good surface for practicing this throw.

The Ninth Day

For those who wish to concentrate on throwing techniques a new method of practicing may now be used. When the partners take turns moving into position for a throw without saying in advance which one they are going to use, it is called Give and Take Practice. The partner who is being thrown should work as actively at falling properly as his partner does at throwing properly. The throwing partner should always finish in a strong balanced "T" position; the partner who is receiving should end in a good protected position. Compare your positions with the photos to check the endings and then correct any mistakes.

LESSON OUTLINE

Review Instruction:

Falls No. 1 through 5
Grab-Defense—Thumb Release (p. 91)
Wrist Holds No. 1 and 2 (p. 66, 76)
Where and How to Strike—Lessons for Fifth through
   Eighth Days
Fist-Fighting Defense—Long-Range Fist Attack (p. 94)
Bent-Arm Hip Throw—Throwing and Receiving (p. 82)
Neck-Lock Hip Throw—Throwing and Receiving (p. 96)

New Instruction:

Grab Defense—Thumb Release and Arm Lock
Where and How to Strike:
   1. The Calf Blow—Toe Kick
   2. The Tendon Blow—Heel Kick
   3. The Inside-of-the-Upper-Thigh Blow—Hooking Kick
Front-Choke Defense No. 1
Captured-Arm Hip Throw—Basic Steps (Balance Only)
Stick or Club Defense—Overhead Attack

Don't Forget . . .

GRAB DEFENSE—Thumb Release and Arm Lock

This defense, a continuation from the previous lesson, gives you a complete defense technique. It is possible that the thumb release alone will be sufficient; if not, you may use the arm lock for a finish.

1. Use the thumb release technique described on page 91. Extend your opponent's held hand and push it across his body.

2. Turn his extended arm so that his elbow is up and begin to pull it under your left arm.

3. As you take a step in with your left foot, continue to pull his arm and clamp it firmly under your arm. Your upper arm should hold his upper arm into your body.

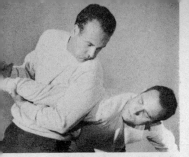

4. This is a close-up of the technique. Note that your opponent's arm is completely extended and held tightly into your body at the upper arm. You should be leaning back slightly but not on your opponent. For additional painful pressure, you should release the thumb, place your right hand on the back of his held hand, and push back.

5. To apply full pressure, raise his held wrist and, using leverage, press on his upper arm. Now with both of your hands raise his held hand up and toward your head. With this action you can take your opponent to the ground.

WHERE AND HOW TO STRIKE

1. The Calf Blow. You can kick forcefully at the calf without fear of doing serious injury. A heavy kick can cause a cramp in the leg muscle and temporarily put your opponent out of action.

2. Under usual circumstances, you will be wearing shoes. Using the toe gives excellent penetration. The drawback to this type of kick is that more accuracy is required than when you use an edge-of-the-foot kick. If you are barefoot, use the ball of your foot when kicking.

3. The Tendon Blow. Strike just above the heel. Serious injury is unlikely, but striking at the tendon will hamper your adversary's foot action.

4. Kicking with the heel of the shoe is an effective method. As you practice the variety of kicks at all areas, you will find that the heel kick is ideal when your adversary is behind you. For kicking into the tendon, the side-of-the-shoe kick is also recommended.

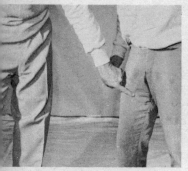

5. The Inside-of-the-Upper-Thigh Blow. There is a heavy concentration of nerves in this area, and a full-power kick can temporarily paralyze the leg. A moderate blow is very painful.

6. A hook-type kick using the toe, a knee kick, or a hand blow using the extended knuckle is effective in this area.

I do not advocate kicking into the groin. A man instinctively protects himself there, and a street fighter will anticipate the kick and put up a good defense against it. He will not so easily anticipate your other kicks and will be less able to handle them. There are many other more readily accessible striking areas which do not involve the danger of serious and permanent injury, yet effectively subdue your adversary.

FRONT–CHOKE DEFENSE NO. 1

Among the common attacks for which we will teach specific defenses are the front choking types of attack. Although the defenses will be referred to as defenses against choking, they are useful for many other reaching types of attack.

Remember that this is not a punching defense but a reaching defense. Whether your adversary intends to choke you, grab you with both hands, or pull or push you, you can use this defense. It is always best to react before your adversary actually has his hands on you.

1. The attacking partner, shown at the right, chokes the defending partner with a straight-arm choke.

2. The defending partner clasps his hands together without interlacing his fingers, holding his elbows out slightly, and bringing his hands up with force between his adversary's arms.

3. This is a close-up of the essential action. The defender's hands come up directly between his opponent's elbows, his forearms striking his opponent's forearms to effect release.

4. The defender carries through so that his clasped hands are high at the completion of the action.

5. The defender follows the release by retaliating with a clasped-hands blow onto his opponent's nose. When practicing, the defender should only simulate the retaliating blow, because receiving the actual blow is painful. In use, full power should be used to break the choke, and a crashing downward blow to retaliate.

CAPTURED–ARM HIP THROW—Basic Steps (Balance Only)

Even when no cloth is available for gripping, this type of hip throw is effective. You must learn to do the throw when you have an opponent who is not dressed for your convenience. After doing this throw as shown, practice it when your partner is not wearing a jacket.

The partners start in a natural stance, facing each other. The partner shown at the right does the throwing.

1. The thrower steps across, starting to pivot. His right hand is in a position to swing under the receiver's right arm.

2. The thrower completes his pivot and grips the cloth at the receiver's right arm just below the shoulder.

3. The thrower bends his knees to place his hip low on the receiver's thigh, and leans the upper part of his body left.

4. By straightening his legs and pulling forward with both arms, the thrower can pull the receiver onto his hip.

STICK OR CLUB DEFENSE—Overhead Attack

A stick extends the attacking arm and is usually part of a long-range attack. The stick, club, or similar weapon is less dangerous when you are close to it than when you step back; therefore, this defense is based on stepping into your opponent. This is one of the very rare situations in which stepping in close to the adversary is recommended.

1. The adversary, shown at the right, attacks with an overhand blow.

2. The defending partner steps in, crosses his arms over his head, firmly locks his forearms, and blocks the attacker's wrist.

3. After blocking the blow, the defending partner grips the attacker's wrist with his right hand.

4. The defender pulls the captured arm down and extends it, turning the attacker's elbow up and stepping back with the right foot.

5. The defender applies the Straight-Arm Bar. He may use pushing pressure, as taught earlier, or may smash down on the elbow. Use of a stick or a club would indicate a vicious attack, one which would justify the more severe retaliation.

DON'T FORGET

• In Give and Take Practice the partners should not "strong-arm" each other but work smoothly and with as little muscular effort as possible.

• Thumb Release and Arm Lock: Pull the attacker's arm out straight, and clamp it firmly into the side of your body.

• Front-Choke Defense: You must spread your arms enough to act as a wedge. The releasing blow should start low and end high.

• Stick Defense: Keep your eye on the weapon, and step in deep under it. Keep your forearms locked firmly as you block the blow.

• Captured-Arm Hip Throw: It is common error to attempt to pull your opponent over your head. The direction in which he moves is across your upper arm. Only in the movies, where the villain is paid a good salary, is it possible to throw the bad guy spectacularly over the head. If you try it in real life, you will find your partner draped awkwardly on your back.

The Tenth Day

How you *think* about your training is as important as how you *train*. A mental review of the techniques you are learning will prepare you for using them on the street. You should imagine various situations and mentally review the defenses you would use. Think of street defenses as being divided into two categories: (1) the simple defenses appropriate to situations that are simply annoying, and (2) the stronger defenses and retaliation justified by serious attacks. As you distinguish between these situations, you will find yourself making proper responses in your training practice.

LESSON OUTLINE

Review Instruction:

Falls No. 1 through 5
Grab-Defense—Thumb Release and Arm Lock (p. 98)
Front-Choke Defense No. 1 (p. 101)
Where and How to Strike—Lessons for Sixth through
    Ninth Days
Stick or Club Defense—Overhead Attack (p. 104)
Fist-Fighting Defense—Long-Range Fist Attack (p. 94)
Bent-Arm Hip Throw—Throwing and Receiving (p. 82)
Neck-Lock Hip Throw—Throwing and Receiving (p. 88)
Captured-Arm Hip Throw—(Balance Only) (p. 103)

New Instruction:

Finger Pressure and Arm Lock
Where and How to Strike:
    1. The Inside-of-the-Lower-Thigh Blow—The Bottom
       of the Foot
    2. The Kneecap Blow—Heel Kick
    3. The Side-of-the-Knee Blow—45° Angle Kick
Front-Choke Defense No. 2
Sixth Fall—Forward Roll to Standing Position
Captured-Arm Hip Throw—Completing the Throw and
    Receiving

Don't Forget . . .

FINGER PRESSURE AND ARM LOCK

This is one of the simplest and most practical techniques possible. It is intended for use when the attack is not violent and will subdue an annoying or bullying opponent who is reaching out to push, pull, or grab you.

1. The attacking partner, shown at the right, reaches out. The defending partner slashes into the forearm nerve center.

2. The slash should weaken the attacker's arm, allowing the defender to grip his fingers with the right hand, almost as though to shake hands. However, only the fingers, not the full hand, are grabbed.

3. The defender turns the attacker's hand palm up. With his left hand he grips the attacker's wrist. With both hands he pulls the attacker's arm straight and raises it, bending the fingers back.

4. Full pressure is applied by continuing to bend the attacker's fingers back as the defender places his left elbow under the attacker's elbow. Both the defender's hands hold the captured hand firm. The defender may walk his opponent backward in this hold if he wishes to.

5. & 6. Ordinarily, this technique will control and end a simple attack. If the attacker becomes more belligerent, the defender may continue in this fashion: raising his arm, still maintaining finger pressure, he steps around clockwise with his right foot, placing himself at his opponent's side, with his back toward him, as in Photo No. 6. The defender applies pressure by levering his arm down and across his own body. He then raises his left shoulder under the attacker's armpit.

WHERE AND HOW TO STRIKE

1. The Inside-of-the-Lower-Thigh Blow. The effect of striking here is the same as for the upper thigh area.

2. Strike at the arch with the bottom of your foot. If the foot is held horizontal, you will have a greater chance of hitting the target, even though you may not do so with perfect accuracy.

3. The Kneecap Blow. Kicking into the knee or kneecap is extremely effective for immobilizing an adversary. Approximately 65 pounds of striking force will dislocate the knee joint. Even a frail person has enough kicking power to stop a much larger and stronger opponent.

4. The Side-of-the-Knee Blow. Kick with the bottom of your foot into the knee, using a 45° angle for best result.

5. Kick at the kneecap with a stamping kick, using your heel. If the attack is from the rear, this is a good kick, although a more precise aim is required for an effective blow.

FRONT–CHOKE DEFENSE NO. 2

Four defenses will be given for use against a front choke and similar attacks. After practicing all of them, choose the one you like best and concentrate on learning to react with speed and precision.

1. The attacking partner, shown at the right, chokes with a straight-arm choke. The defending partner raises both his hands for a side-of-the-hand blow.

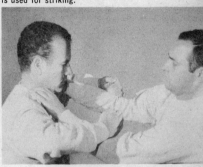

3. This photo shows a close-up of the blow. The hands are kept firm but not rigid. The thumb is held against the side of the hand. The fleshy part of the edge of the hand is used for striking.

2. The defender smashes down on the forearm nerve center. In practice stop just short of actual hitting.

4. After effecting a release, the defender can strike into any of the nerve centers in the upper body. A fingertip stab into the neck muscle is shown.

SIXTH BASIC FALL—Forward Roll to Standing Position

The function of this fall is to prepare you for learning more advanced rolling falls.

The starting and ending positions for this fall are the same: Standing in a relaxed stance, the feet shoulder-width apart, the weight distributed equally on both feet.

1. Fold your arms and place them on your head to protect it. Squat low to the ground. Tuck your head in.

2. Place your folded arms on the ground, as close to your feet as possible, throwing your weight forward. As you begin your roll, push with your feet to assist your forward motion.

3. As you start to come out of the roll, fling your arms straight out to give you momentum to continue up into a standing position.

1. Execute the throw with three simultaneous motions: (a) spring up onto the balls of your feet; (b) pull down and around (describing a circle) with both arms; and (c) rotate your upper body to follow and assist your arm motion.

2. Until the receiver is experienced in taking the fall, the thrower should maintain a firm grip with both hands on the receiver's right sleeve or arm, being sure to pull up to ease the action of the fall. The thrower should check and correct the ending position of the receiver.

DON'T FORGET

· Finger Pressure and Arm Lock: If you cannot grasp all the fingers, grasp at least two. Use your body to apply pressure against them. Be very careful when practicing, but in actual use you may use a snapping action.

· Front-Choke Defense: The fingers of the striking hands are held together. Avoid striking with the bony portion of the side of your hand.

· Sixth Fall: Don't leap or jump into this fall; roll into it.

1. Falling techniques which require that you slap the mat to absorb shock are timed so that the slap is done:
   A. Just **before** the body hits the mat.
   B. Just **as** the body hits the mat.
   C. Just **after** the body hits the mat.
2. When executing the Hip Throw:
   A. Only the arms are used.
   B. The arms are used for pulling as you twist your body and spring up.
   C. The arms describe a circle, and the feet remain firmly on the ground.
3. A small person can escape from a wrist-grab because of:
   A. Muscle reaction.
   B. Deception and distraction.
   C. Reflex action.
4. For a complete fist-fighting defense, the order of action against the oncoming attack is:
   A. Block the attack; weaken the opponent; throw.
   B. Move in to meet the attack; employ all methods of defense and attack until the opponent is subdued.
   C. Use long-range kicks; block the blows before retaliating.
5. A blow delivered into the solar plexus in an upper direction should be used only:
   A. Late at night, on a dark street.
   B. In case of a violent attack.
   C. If you are bigger than your opponent.
6. For safety, the proper ending of the Fifth Fall is:
   A. Head up, hip down; slap at sides of the body; hands and feet slapping simultaneously.
   B. Shoulders and feet touching the mat, legs straight; slap at sides.
   C. Hands and feet slap simultaneously; hip and head up.

7. The long-range fist attack allows you to take a defensive position:
    A. Before you rush your opponent to apply your defense.
    B. Before you turn and run.
    C. Before your opponent is within striking range.
8. When you are attacked with a stick or club, your best action is:
    A. Move out of range; block the attack; apply an arm lock.
    B. Move in close to your opponent; block and counter.
    C. Leap up; grab the club; twist it out of his grip.
9. Kicking into the knee is a good defense against a serious attack. At what angle should you kick for best results? How much pressure is normally required to dislocate the knee if it is kicked at the proper angle?
    A. At a 45° angle, 65 pounds of pressure.
    B. At a 90° angle, 45 pounds of pressure.
    C. At a 45° angle, 90 pounds of pressure.
10. Safety measures must be observed when practicing throws. A beginner should be thrown with special care. As an important safety measure, the thrower should:
    A. Keep one arm held tight around the receiver's neck and pull up so that the head does not touch the mat.
    B. Tell the receiver, just before he hits the mat, to relax and slap the mat with force.
    C. Maintain a firm grip on the receiver's sleeve and lapel to ease the fall.

Answers on page 224.

The Eleventh Day

You are now at the half-way point in your training and should be aware of those techniques which are most suitable for you and those which you can eliminate. As this decision will be different for each individual, partners should not attempt to influence each other. Since you are being shown many more techniques than you will ever need for practical defense, it is wise for you to choose those which work best for you and intensify your training in them.

LESSON OUTLINE

Review Instruction:

Falls No. 1 through 6
Reverse Arm Lock (p. 84)
Finger Pressure and Arm Lock (p. 107)
Grab-Defense—Thumb Release and Arm Lock (p. 98)
Front-Choke Defenses No. 1 and 2 (p. 101, 110)
Where and How to Strike—Lessons for Seventh through
    Tenth Days
Stick or Club Defense—Overhead Attack (p. 104)
Neck-Lock Hip Throw—Throwing and Receiving (p. 96)
Captured-Arm Hip Throw—Throwing and Receiving
    (p. 113)

New Instruction:

Front-Choke Defense No. 3
Where and How to Strike:
    1. The Shinbone Blow—Edge-of-the-Shoe Kick
    2. The Instep Blow—Stamping Kick
    3. The Anklebone Blow—Edge-of-the-Shoe Kick
Fist-Fighting Defense: Close-In Attack—Block and
    Simultaneous Blows with Take-down
Straight-Leg Throw—Basic Steps (Position Only)

Don't Forget . . .

FRONT–CHOKE DEFENSE NO. 3

1. The attacking partner, shown at the right, chokes with the straight-arm choke.

2. & 3. Striking with the heels of his palms, the defending partner hits sharply at his opponent's wrists. A close-up is shown in Photo No. 3. At the beginning of practice, the defender strikes with one hand and follows quickly with the other. With progress, blows should be struck with both hands simultaneously. The hands should be cupped with the fingers held together.

4. The defender follows through with a snappy action in order to force the attacker's hands out.

5. The defender retaliates with simultaneous edge-of-the-hand slashes into his opponent's neck.

WHERE AND HOW TO STRIKE

1. The Shinbone Blow. The shinbone extends from the knee to the instep and because it is extremely sensitive it is an excellent target for kicking. Even a moderate blow causes great pain and a heavy blow can incapacitate an adversary. In spite of this there is no danger of permanent serious injury. It has the additional advantage of being an easy, accessible target, very difficult for your adversary to defend.

2. An outside edge-of-the-shoe blow to the shin is ideal. Follow through by scraping down the length of the shin.

3. The Instep Blow. The top of the foot is the target area. A moderate blow can cause great pain and will hinder the ability to walk. A heavy kick can break the small bones in the arch of the foot.

4. The blow is delivered by stamping down with the arch or with the heel of the shoe.

5. The Anklebone Blow. The kick should be delivered to the top of the round bone at the outside of the foot and also at the inside of the foot. Kicks to this area are very painful, although there is little danger of injury from even a heavy kick. The pain will often stop an attack or distract the attacker and allow the defender to continue a subduing defense.

6. This shows a kick with the outside edge of the shoe. Many of the foot blows are effective in this area.

FIST–FIGHTING DEFENSE: Close-in Attack—Block and Simultaneous Blows with Take-down

Quick response is essential for defending against a fist attack close in. The fist-fighting defenses which you have already learned are useful in situations where you have had some warning of the attack. In a rushing and out-of-fist range attack, you will have time to respond with your strongest defense first—kicking. In a close-in fist-fighting attack, there is less likelihood of forewarning, and practice in blocking blows (as shown in Photo No. 1) becomes the basic element in building a good defense.

1. The attacking partner hits out with one or both fists. The exact type of attack is not important. The defending partner should block both arms with his forearms. As he improves the defending partner should try blocking with a side-of-the-hand blow. If the attacking partner hits with only one fist, the defender blocks that arm and gets in a position to block the second blow. Blocking should not be done across the body; the attacker's right arm is always blocked by the defender's left arm, and vice versa. With practice, the defender will respond automatically to a fist blow by blocking. Attacking partner, right.

2. & 3. After blocking, the defender retaliates immediately with three simultaneous blows. It is important to use THREE blows. The average person might be able to stop one retaliating blow; a trained fighter can stop two blows; but no one can cope with three simultaneous blows! The photos show two combinations of triple blows. Any of several combinations may be practiced. It is best to strike into three separate areas: hit high with one hand, into the middle with the other hand and low with the kick.

4. After weakening or stunning his adversary, the defender grabs the attacker's lead arm and spins him around so that his back is toward the defender.

5. If necessary, the defender can grip the attacker's collar firmly and continue striking.

6. Kicking into the back of the attacker's knee and pulling down on his collar will take him to the ground.

1. Partners stand facing each other, holding at the sleeve and lapel in the usual starting position.

2. The thrower, shown at the right, turns his left foot so that it points away from the receiver at a 45° angle.

3. Putting his weight on his left foot, the thrower raises his right foot. As he does this, he pulls the receiver into a weak balance position by pulling forward at the receiver's right sleeve and pushing back at the receiver's left lapel.

4. The thrower places his right foot (ankle-to-ankle) at the receiver's right foot. The thrower bends his left leg slightly but keeps his right leg firm and straight. As the thrower places his foot down, he continues the arm action, pulling the receiver in the direction of his chest, further weakening the receiver's balance. Throughout the action most of the thrower's weight is on his left foot.

DON'T FORGET

• **Front-Choke Defense:** Keep your thumbs alongside of your hand. If you allow the thumbs to point out, you may hurt them. The direction of the snappy blow is slightly upward.

• **Fist-Fighting Defense:** In your training be sure that you YELL as you hit! As soon as you have visibly weakened your adversary, spin him around. The faster you place him with his back to you, the easier it is to finish the defense.

• **Straight-Leg Throw:** Your ankle should be locked to your opponent's ankle with your right leg straight and stiff. Lean far to the left with the upper part of your body.

The Twelfth Day

Judo, Karate, and Jujitsu methods have been effective for thousands of years and properly applied they will work for you. Never try to show what you know merely to satisfy the curiosity of your friends. The techniques are for actual use and cannot really be demonstrated without the strong possibility of your hurting someone. These methods of self-defense are not a game and should always be treated with respect.

LESSON OUTLINE

Review Instruction:

Falls No. 1 through 6
Front-Choke Defenses Nos. 1, 2, 3 (p. 101, 110, 117)
Where and How to Strike—Lessons for Eighth through
    Eleventh Days
Stick or Club Defense—Overhead Attack (p. 104)
Neck-Lock Hip Throw—Throwing and Receiving (p. 96)
Captured-Arm Hip Throw—Throwing and Receiving
    (p. 113)
Straight-Leg Throw (Position Only) (p. 122)

New Instruction:

Front-Choke Defense No. 4
Stick or Club Defense—Side Blow
Seventh Fall—Side Roll and Come Up
Straight-Leg Throw—Completion of Throw and Receiving

Don't Forget . . .

FRONT–CHOKE DEFENSE NO. 4

With this defense you will have been given four defenses against a front choke and similar attacks. Practice each of the four until you are certain which are best for your style of work, and then concentrate on them.

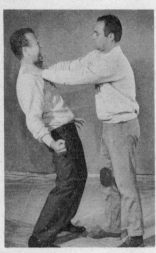

1. The attacking partner, shown at the right, applies a straight-arm choke.

2. With your hands cupped, press in at his elbows, holding your elbows high.

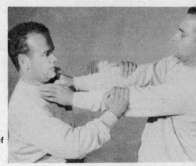

3. This is a close-up. Pressing in at his elbows (the weakest part of the grip) stops the choking pressure.

4. Continue pressing his elbows, and push him back with a continuous action.

5. Grip the cloth at his elbows, and raise his arms as you step in front of him with your left foot.

6. To trip him forward maintain your grip on his arms, and pull him over. You may take him down by continuing the forward pull, keeping your left leg firm and straight, and twisting your body down and around to your right.

1. By the way he holds his stick or club, you can tell that the attacker is getting ready to swing in a wild, roundhouse action.

2. Step far in with your left foot to get inside the weapon. With the center of your forearms block his striking arm at his upper arm and his forearm.

3. Grip his wrist with your left hand. At this point, if he still resists, kick into his lower leg to distract and weaken him.

4. Take a second long step in with your right foot as you reach under his held arm with your right arm. Place the bony part of your right forearm at the nerve center about 4 inches above his elbow at the back of his arm, and apply pressure by pulling forward with your right arm as you push on his held wrist with your left hand.

5. If you find it necessary to take him down from this position, place your right leg in a Straight-Leg Throw position, throwing him back over your leg. The throw is effected by pulling him around, back, and down with your left hand, and by pushing him with your right arm and shoulder.

SEVENTH FALL—Side Roll and Come Up

Rolling and coming up is excellent for exercising and for safety practice. If you plan to continue in Sport Judo it is essential to do this fall properly or if you and your partner merely wish to emphasize throwing techniques for self-defense.

Falling techniques present a special difficulty for some students. Do not be discouraged if you are among them. There are many people who never learn the falls completely and yet have a great proficiency in street defense.

1. Starting position. Take one step forward with your left foot. Place your hands in position to touch the mat in the following manner. The fingers of your left hand are pointed toward you and your left elbow is pointed away from you; your right hand is held next to your left hand with the fingers pointed in the direction of the roll; your arms are held firm, forming a circle. If you think of your arms as being a wheel over which you are rolling the rest of your body, you will have the proper idea of this fall.

2. Place your hands on the mat, tuck your head in, shift your weight toward your left foot and hand, raise your right leg, and start to lose your balance over your left shoulder. Do not fling yourself forward. This should be an easy roll over.

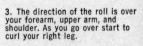

3. The direction of the roll is over your forearm, upper arm, and shoulder. As you go over start to curl your right leg.

Although this fall is done as a smooth continuous motion, it is not necessary for good form to do it fast. The slap should be done *as* you roll.

4. As you complete this roll, your right leg should be tucked in, your left foot ready to touch the mat, and your right hand getting ready to slap.

5. The roll is completed. The slap should absorb the impact and help to drive you up onto your feet.

6. Finish in a standing position, turning to face the spot where you started the fall. Assume a strong balance stance.

STRAIGHT-LEG THROW—Completion of Throw and Receiving

1. To place the receiver in position for the throw, the thrower pulls him into his chest and locks him there with his arms. His right leg is kept firmly locked at the receiver's right leg, ankle-to-ankle.

2. To execute the throw, the thrower twists the receiver's body sharply, causing him to trip over the thrower's locked leg.

3. In the early stages of practice the thrower helps the receiver by maintaining a grip on his lapel and sleeve.

4. With more advanced training, the thrower may release his lapel grip when the throw is executed, but should maintain his sleeve grip throughout practice. The thrower should check and correct the ending position of the receiver.

DON'T FORGET

• Front-Choke Defense: Don't let your thumbs point down; keep them next to your forefingers. Keep your elbows high. Press *in* first and then *away* in a continuous action.

• Stick Defense: Block *both* the forearm and the upper arm, not just one of them. Step far in with your left foot. Don't block the stick, block the arm.

• Seventh Fall: Keep your arms rounded and firm. If you allow your arms to collapse as you touch the mat, you will bang your shoulder. Tuck your head in to avoid touching the mat. Curl your legs to assist you in rising to your feet.

• Straight-Leg Throw: To break your opponent's balance, pull him in to your chest *first;* then twist his body and finish the throw.

The Thirteenth Day

You may not always be in a position to defend yourself from your strong side so you should practice all self-defense techniques with both the right and the left hands as well as against right- and left-handed attacks. Learn to use both the hands and the feet for striking simultaneously. True versatility comes from utilizing both, rather than from learning a great number of techniques.

LESSON OUTLINE

Review Instruction:

Falls No. 1, 2, 3, 6, 7
Front-Choke Defenses No. 1 through 4 (p. 101, 110, 117, 126)
Straight-Arm Bar (p. 32)
Pushing Defense (p. 42)
Back-Choke Defense—Finger Grip (p. 50)
Stick or Club Defense—Side Blow (p. 128)
Captured-Arm Hip Throw—Throwing and Receiving (p. 113)
Straight-Leg Throw—Throwing and Receiving (p. 132)

New Instruction:

Arm-Pin Defense—Back Attack
Knife Defense—Stabbing Attack
Fist-Fighting Defense—Parry and Forward Trip
Sitting-Down Throw—Basic Steps (Position Only)

Don't Forget . . .

ARM–PIN DEFENSE—Back Attack

2. Weaken the attacker with hand and foot blows. Shown in this photo are the bottom of the foot stamping back into the shin or knee and a side-of-the-hand slash into the thigh. For this action you can use a number of other blows which you have already learned, for instance edge-of-the-shoe kicking into the shin and scraping down, stamping onto the instep, etc.

1. The attacking partner, shown at the left, grabs you from the rear and pins your arms.

3. & 4. When you have sufficiently weakened your adversary so that his grip is less strong, turn to one side. This will further weaken his grip on the side to which you turn. Although it may increase the strength of his grip on your other arm, it will allow you to slide the captured arm out of his grip, as shown in Photo No. 4.

5. Strike back with an elbow blow into the attacker's face. This should effect a complete release.

6. Turn to face your adversary. Be ready to follow through with additional blows if necessary to subdue him.

KNIFE DEFENSE—Stabbing Attack

If a man threatens you with a knife, he probably intends to kill or maim you. A person who carries a knife is usually experienced in how to use it, so DON'T try to block, grab, parry, or grapple with him. This defense may be used against other cutting weapons, such as an ice pick, a beer-can opener, a broken bottle, etc. If you can, throw something at your adversary or strike him with a chair or anything else handy, and run away if possible. If, however, you are in a confined area or your adversary is in very close, you must make a defense!

1. Your partner threatens you with a knife. A rubber knife should always be used for practice.

2. As your adversary starts to stab, push off with your right foot, taking a long leap to the side of the attacking hand. If you leap in the opposite direction, his arm movement can follow you more easily. A leap at a 45° angle is best, and will place you to the side and slightly to the rear of your adversary.

3. The leap and the kick which follows are a continuous action. As soon as you land on your left foot, kick with great force with your right foot at the attacker's right knee. Practice for a quick leap and kick so that your foot blow reaches his knee before he can turn to face your new position.

One kick, with all your force, could stop the attack, but you must continue with kicks, moving around to his back, until you are certain that he is subdued.

After you have practiced the defense as described above, execute it in the following manner: At the first sign of attack, leap straight back. This action will draw the attacker out, revealing the exact style and motion of his knife thrust. At the second stab, leap to the side and execute the kick swiftly and with force.

FIST–FIGHT DEFENSE—Parry and Forward Trip

Parrying is useful when the fist attack is made from out of striking range. A parry defense is especially useful against a powerful adversary as you divert the power of the attacker's fist, rather than stop it.

1. When the threat of a fist attack is made out of fist range it means that your adversary cannot hit you unless he takes at least one step in. First assume a street-fighting stance. I have found that a great number of threats of attack are stopped when the fighting stance is taken because the street fighter ordinarily fights only those he feels he can easily beat. He may be confused and distracted from his purpose by the sight of this intended victim preparing to fight him in a style with which he is unfamiliar.

2. As the attacker strikes out, step to the side, and dodge with your body to avoid the blow. At the same time, strike against his forearm with the palm of your hand, changing the direction of his blow. Use a snappy action to parry.

3. Retaliate immediately by striking with any of your hand blows. Shown is an open-hand blow to the side of the neck.

4. Because of your parrying action, the attacker will probably be offbalance. Grip the cloth at his right shoulder and move him along in the direction of his own forward movement. Simultaneously, kick into his shin with your right foot. Using the bottom of your foot is most effective, but a side-of-the-shoe kick can also be used.

5. & 6. The combination of the tripping kick and the forward pulling motion should take the attacker down. When you feel that he is falling, place your right foot down firmly and get into a strong, balanced position, as in Photo No. 6. The attacker should now be completely under control. If necessary, be ready to continue with hand and foot blows.

SITTING–DOWN THROW—Basic Steps (Position Only)

1. The partners assume the basic stance for starting the throw. Thrower, left.

2. The thrower sidesteps with his left foot, pointing it toward the receiver at a 45° angle.

3. The thrower turns his body clockwise a quarter turn, pulling the receiver off balance as he places his right foot on the receiver's left instep.

4. The thrower sits down off to the side, not in front of the receiver, and, as he sits down, pulls the receiver down and forward.

Because this throw places you on the ground, it is recommended for street defense only when you are in danger of being pushed down anyway, or when your adversary is leaning so far forward that it is easy to throw him. It is a simple throw because you do not support his weight while doing it.

DON'T FORGET

• **Arm-Pin Defense:** Do not attempt a release until your adversary is noticeably weakened. Turn to face him quickly when you are released.

• **Parrying Fist-Fighting Attack:** Make sure you move your head and body out of range of the attacking fist. Practice the first part of this defense on both sides (right- and left-hand attacks) until you can quickly and easily parry blows. The proper parry is the essential part of the defense.

• **Knife Defense:** Don't jump to the side prematurely. If you jump before he has attacked, the attacker will simply turn to face you in your new position. Don't move in to your adversary or try to take the knife away until you have subdued him with kicking blows.

• **Sitting-Down Throw:** Do not sit down directly in front of your opponent for the throw. Step to the side so that you will avoid having him fall on top of you. Keep your foot firmly placed high on his instep. As you lower yourself, bring him down with you. If you keep your arms extended as the throw is begun, it will allow your opponent to remain standing. If you keep your arms bent and in close to your body, he must follow your action as you go down.

The Fourteenth Day

Before beginning this lesson, re-read the chapter of "Preliminary Instructions." It will be of value to refresh your mind on some of the important elements in this training.

LESSON OUTLINE

Review Instruction:

Falls No. 1, 2, 3, 6, 7
Front-Choke Defenses No. 3 and 4 (p. 117, 126)
Arm-Pin Defense—Back Attack (p. 135)
Fist-Fighting Defense: Close-in Attack—Block and
      Simultaneous Blows with Take-down (p. 120)
Parry and Forward Trip (p. 138)
Knife Defense—Stabbing Attack (p. 136)
Straight-Leg Throw—Throwing and Receiving (p. 132)
Sitting-Down Throw (Position Only) (p. 140)

New Instruction:

Back-Grab Defense—Under Arms
Knife Defense—Slashing Attack
Eighth Fall—Standing and Fall on Side
Sitting-Down Throw—Completion of Throw and Receiving

Don't Forget . . .

BACK–GRAB DEFENSE—Under Arms

It is always assumed that your adversary is stronger and larger than you are. Therefore to try to struggle out of his grip would be useless.

1. The attacking partner grips you around the waist, leaving your arms free.

2. & 3. Jab into the back of the attacker's hand nerve center with an extended knuckle blow, and at the same time kick into his shin. It may require several kicks to weaken him so that he partially loosens his hold. When you feel the grip loosen, clasp your hands together (do not interlace your fingers), turn to see your target, and strike at his face with an elbow blow to effect a complete release (Photo No. 3.).

KNIFE DEFENSE—Slashing Attack

The main difference in your defense against a slashing attack and a stabbing attack is the direction of your leap.

1. Your adversary's posture will indicate that he is preparing to slash rather than stab with his weapon.

2. As he begins the sweeping motion, leap back by pushing with your lead foot and jump out of range of the weapon, landing on your rear foot.

3. Lean your upper body well back and out of range. After the weapon has passed you, kick the attacker's knee with your lead foot. Timing is important. Your kick should be delivered after his slashing arm has gone by you and before he can recover to attack again. Your first kick may not disable him, but it will at least distract him from his attack enough to allow you to deliver a second kick. Do not attempt to grab, block, parry, or grapple with the knife hand until you have definitely weakened your adversary.

When you have practiced the defense as taught above, you should practice leaping back once to draw out your adversary and then begin your kicking defense after the second leap.

EIGHTH FALL—Standing and Fall on Side

This advanced form of falling onto your side is a good safety fall. If you fall, or are pushed, trip or slip on a hard surface, executing this fall could save you a broken bone. Slapping the ground as you fall absorbs the shock of the initial impact. Though slapping the sidewalk will sting your hand, that is preferable to a broken arm.

1. Standing in a relaxed stance, point your left foot to the side.

2. Shift your weight to your left foot, bring your right leg up across your body, and swing your right hand up.

. Lower yourself, bending your ʔft knee as if preparing to sit ʔose to your left heel. Your right ʔand should continue its swing up.

4. When you are as close to the mat as you can be without falling, gently roll back on your right side. As your hip touches the mat, your right hand slaps. Your feet should be raised and your head should not touch the mat.

Do not thrust or drive yourself to the ground. The action should be continuous and easy. Smoothness is essential.

SITTING-DOWN THROW—Completion of Throw and Receiving

1. The thrower executes the throw by continuing the downward pull with his arms. Note: This throw must be practiced in slow motion at the beginning. The thrower will not actually throw, but will go through the motions while the receiver carefully prepares to fall properly.

2. The receiving partner places his hands on the mat as in the Seventh Fall, tucking his head in and rolling over his arms. The throwing partner, in beginning practice, does not fling the receiving partner over, but assists him by guiding him over. In actual use, the thrower thrusts with his arms and kicks up and over with his right foot.

3. & 4. The receiving partner continues the motion of the Seventh Fall, ending by slapping the ground, curling his legs, and, using the momentum of the roll, comes up on his feet in a standing position.

DON'T FORGET

· Back-Grab Defense: Bend forward slightly for the elbow blow and turn your head to see your target.

· Knife Defense: Emphasize leaping practice to build up the distance you can leap. As you may have to leap twice before kicking, you should be sure to land in a well-balanced position.

· Eighth Fall: Don't fall from a standing position. Ease yourself down as low as possible before rolling. Don't let your head touch the ground. Fall on your side, not on your back. Keep your arm extended for the slap; do not bend it or you will fall on your elbow.

· Sitting-Down Throw: Sit to the side of your partner. Do not pull your partner down on top of you, but off to the opposite side.

The Fifteenth Day

You should be able to defend yourself even when you do not have the use of your hands. To help develop this versatility, create a handicap for yourself by putting your hands behind your back (gripping your waist band). As your partner simulates a fist attack, leap back, kick at his legs, and circle to his rear. Keep moving, continuing your kicks, so that you are behind him. A moving target is harder to hit, and you are in position for strong defense.

LESSON OUTLINE

Review Instruction:

Falls No. 1, 2, 3, 7, 8
Arm-Pin Defense—Back Attack (p. 135)
Back-Grab Defense—Under Arms (p. 143)
Reverse Arm Lock (p. 84)
Finger Pressure and Arm Lock (p. 107)
Fist-Fighting Defense—Parry and Forward Trip (p. 138)
Knife Defense—Stabbing and Slashing Attacks (p. 136, 144)
Straight-Leg Throw—Throwing and Receiving (p. 132)
Sitting-Down Throw—Throwing and Receiving (p. 146)

New Instruction:

Close-In Fist-Fighting Defense—Block, Leap, Kick, and Choke
Over-Arm Lock
Circle Throw—Basic Steps (Position Only)

Don't Forget . . .

CLOSE–IN FIST–FIGHTING DEFENSE—Block, Leap, Kick, and Choke

Because kicking is best against a serious attack and because it is always better to stay out of fist range, your first choice of defense even in close quarters should be the procedure taught below. Needless to say, if you are not able to leap back after blocking your opponent's attack, you must rely on one of the other close-in defense methods.

1. The attacking partner, shown at the right, threatens a fist attack within hitting range.

2. Block both his arms with your forearms, striking from the inside in an outward direction.

3. Leap straight back, pushing off with your lead foot and landing on your rear foot. This leap should take you completely out of his fist range and make it impossible for him to hit you without taking a step in.

4. Immediately kick into the attacker's middle or leg area. In training it is good to practice kicking above the belt area in order to increase your general kicking proficiency. On the street, kick into the knee or below. There will be almost no opportunity for your adversary to catch or block your kick if it is low. Only advanced students should attempt higher kicking techniques in an actual fight.

5. Turn and deliver quickly a second kick into the leg area. There is a good reason for turning your body and using your other foot for the second kick. When you kick a solid object, there is normally a recoil which will tend to knock you off your balance. Deliberately planting the kicking foot on the ground and kicking for the second time with the other foot gives you a stronger stance than if you attempt two kicks with the same foot.

6. When the attacker is visibly weakened, grip his leading arm, and spin him so that his back is toward you.

7. Maintaining your grip on his arm and pulling him back off balance, start the choke restraint with your free arm.

8. To execute the choke, lock your forearm into his throat and grip the cloth at his shoulder. Apply pressure by pulling back and around with your choking arm as you pull his sleeve out to the side.

OVER–ARM LOCK

This is an excellent hold for complete control of an annoying adversary you want to remove from a room. It is not practical to use it against a violent attack.

1. When the attacker, left, reaches out, slash into his forearm nerve center with sufficient force to numb his arm, stepping to his right side with your left foot as you slash.

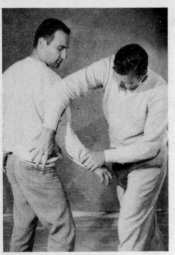

2. With your left hand, grip his right wrist, using a natural grip. Your right hand should reach over his held arm.

3. Continue to reach over his held arm and then around it to grip your own left wrist, using an unnatural grip.

4. Lever his arm up his back, using the action of both your arms; at the same time, turn your body so that you are facing his side.

5. Maintain your hold and step back with your right foot, taking a "T" position.

6. Apply pressure by locking his held arm into your arms and forcing up against his wrist.

At this point you can control your adversary and either walk him wherever you want or take him to the ground by lowering yourself onto your knee. Be very careful because by snapping up with both your arms you can dislocate his shoulder.

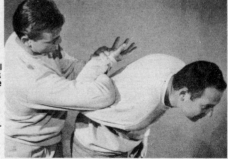

CIRCLE THROW—Basic Steps (Position Only)

As with the Sitting-Down Throw, this throw has the disadvantage of placing you on the ground.

However, it has the same advantage of being easy to apply if your adversary is pushing you back or if you are in danger of losing your balance backward. In that case, you should make the best of the situation by grabbing your adversary and using the Circle Throw.

1. The partners start in a natural stance.

2. The thrower, shown at the left, steps in deep between the receiver's feet. When the thrower is in under the center of gravity of the receiver, it is easier to break his balance.

3. As the thrower starts to sit on the ground, he places his right foot at the receiver's belt.

4. The thrower lowers himself to the ground, sitting as close to his left heel as possible. As he continues down, he pulls the receiver down.

At this point in your training you should not complete the throw. Stop at the point where you are seated and the receiver is leaning well forward.

DON'T FORGET

• Over-Arm Lock: When you reach over the held arm, grab your own wrist. Bend your opponent's held arm with both your arms. When you have the hold, lock it in tight. Maintain a good "T" position.

• Close-In Fist-Fighting Defense: If you have warning of a fist attack, get out of the way before your opponent is in hitting range. If it is a surprise attack, block before leaping. Do not attempt to complete the defense until you have weakened your adversary with kicks.

• Circle Throw: Step in deep between the receiver's feet before you start to sit. Do not drop down to the sitting position abruptly. Sit down easily.

Third Progress Test

1. Blocking should be your first action when threatened by a close-in fist attack. Block in the following manner:
   A. Block your opponent's left arm with your right arm across. Block his right arm with your right arm down.
   B. Block his right arm with your left arm. Block his left arm with your right arm.
   C. Block with your right arm against his right, and with your left arm against his left arm.

2. The Straight-Leg Throw is a tripping type of throw. No body weight need be carried by the thrower, and the throw can be executed at arm's length. For these reasons, the Straight-Leg Throw is particularly useful to these people:
   A. Smaller persons; long-legged persons.
   B. People with long arms and short legs; tall persons with short legs.
   C. Small persons with long arms; persons with thin legs.

3. In the Seventh Fall the direction of the roll is:
   A. Over your neck, across your back, and up on your feet.
   B. Over your forearm, upper arm, and shoulder.
   C. Over your arm, across your shoulder, and onto your back.

4. Defending against a stick attack, side blow, requires that you:
   A. Block the forearm and step in deep with your left foot.
   B. Block his upper arm and step in deep with your right foot.
   C. Block his forearm and his upper arm and step in deep with your left foot.

5. The Parry Fist-Fighting Defense is:
   A. Ideal for use against a very powerful adversary because it can stop the power of his fist.
   B. A defense against a long-range power fist attack.
   C. A defense against a close-in fist attack by which you divert the power of his fist.

6. Don't try to block, grab, parry, or grapple with a knife attacker. The best defense against a knife attack is:
    A. Run away, if at all possible. If you cannot run, kick.
    B. Try to talk yourself out of the situation and call the police.
    C. As soon as you see the danger of attack, rush your attacker and use kicks and slashes.
7. The Sitting-Down Throw is primarily a throw for Sport Judo. Under certain circumstances it may be used to good effect in street defense. One condition for its use in street defense is:
    A. You are sitting on the ground and do not wish to stand up to defend yourself.
    B. You are in danger of being pushed down.
    C. Your opponent is losing his balance backward.
8. The best way to learn throwing techniques is:
    A. Resist as completely as you can your partner's attempts to throw you.
    B. Try the throws on people who do not expect them.
    C. Work slowly getting the feel of each action and learn the proper way to fall as well.
9. When confronted by a belligerent person who wants to fight:
    A. Act meek and cower down. Your adversary will have pity on you.
    B. Attack first. Put up a strong, tough appearance.
    C. Be alert. Fight only if necessary.
10. The parry defense against a long-range fist attack has an advantage over blocking because:
    A. You divert the attack instead of stopping it.
    B. You do not have to make contact with your opponent.
    C. Parrying injures the opponent's arms.

Answers on page 224.

The Sixteenth Day

The first leap out of a danger area can mean a great deal to you when making a defense against the most serious attacks. Practice leaping for distance and for improving your balance when you land.

LESSON OUTLINE

Review Instruction:

Falls No. 1, 2, 3, 7, 8
Over-Arm Lock (p. 152)
Arm-Pin Defense—Back Attack (p. 135)
Back-Grab Defense—Under Arms (p. 143)
Close-in Fist-Fighting Defense—Block, Leap, Kick, and Choke (p. 149)
Knife Defense—Stabbing and Slashing Attacks (p. 136, 144)
Straight-Leg Throw—Throwing and Receiving (p. 132)
Sitting-Down Throw—Throwing and Receiving (p. 146)
Circle Throw (Position Only) (p. 154)

New Instruction:

Back-Grab Defense—Over Arms
Gang-Attack Defense—Front and Back
Circle Throw—Completion of Throw and Receiving

Don't Forget . . .

BACK-GRAB DEFENSE—Over Arms

1. The attacking partner grabs you from the rear, immobilizing your arms.

2. Weaken him by kicking into his shin and slashing into his thigh. This should considerably reduce the power of his grip.

3. Clasp your hands together (do not interlace your fingers) and take a deep breath, forcing your elbows out. This action should break the attacker's grip or expand it enough to allow you to continue this defense.

4. Exhale quickly, turn, and slide down and out from between his arms. Immediately deliver an elbow blow into his solar plexus or abdomen. Then step back and away from your adversary, ready to continue with further hand and foot blows, if necessary.

1. Two opponents threaten to attack you, one on either side

Individuals who lack confidence will attack in a gang. Once you understand the gang members' attitude you will be better able to cope with them. Do not try to reason or plead with a gang, for they would not be attacking a single individual if they were reasonable. The sadistic pleasure which a gang is looking for depends on the helplessness of their intended victim and anyone who puts up the slightest amount of skilled resistance has a good chance of escaping a beating. Fear on the part of the intended victim only increases the sadistic pleasure which they seek; opposition will discourage them. You must attack *first*. Unless you do, you will be attacked simultaneously and find yourself in the worst position possible. You must attack either the end person closest to you, the largest person, or the leader. When you attack, you must move quickly to the outside of the gang. Do not allow yourself to be caught between two people. Do not attack head-on. Attack from the side and work around to the rear. Emphasize kicking and yelling as your most important technique. From reports which have come from my students, many intended gang beatings have been stopped when the intended victim has visibly hurt one person in the gang. Gang members who attack an individual are not brave people, and they do not ordinarily expect to get hurt. If there appears to be a chance that they will get hurt, they may disperse.

2. Use your strongest defense in the direction of your weakest area; in this case it is to the rear. If the opponent to the front is considerably larger, you should kick at him first. For training purposes, kick high. On the street, kick into the shin or knee. Block the arms of the opponent to the front, or slash into the neck or upper area if his arms are not up.

3. After kicking and slashing, reverse your attack and kick low and slash high. It may require several switches of this sort to weaken your two opponents. Do not try the finish until you have first weakened your opponents.

4. & 5. Move to the side of your nearest opponent, grip the cloth at his shoulder or upper arm, and fling him at the other opponent as shown in Photo No. 5.

6. & 7. Leap to the side and continue to kick, first at one opponent and then at the other, as in Photo No. 7, until they are on the ground. Do not try to grapple with them.

Note: Even when you have subdued your opponents, be careful not to walk into a trap as they could have friends nearby. Leave the area as quickly as you can and be on guard.

CIRCLE THROW—Completion of Throw and Receiving

1. The thrower, on the mat, has the receiver in position for completing the Circle Throw. The thrower keeps his knee bent. The receiver has his left foot forward and is leading with his left arm. The hands and arms of the receiver are in position for the Seventh Fall. **Remember:** For the time being the thrower goes through the **motions** only of throwing. The receiver actually takes his own fall until both partners have developed good rolling-fall techniques.

2. Keeping the knee bent the thrower simulates the throwing form by pulling with both his arms very gently over his right shoulder as his foot describes a half circle. The receiver should get ready to place his hands down on the mat and raise his right leg to assist his easy motion over.

3. 4. & 5. The receiver loses his balance and tucks his head in. Photos No. 4 and 5 show the completion of this gentle, rolling fall, and the receiver ready to finish in a standing position. The receiver should be sure that his arms do not buckle but act as a slight prop. His right leg is curled for the proper form of the fall. The head and shoulder of the receiver should not bang the mat, and there should be no sensation of jarring or bumping when the fall is done well. Slow-motion practice is best. Beginning students should guard against the tendency to **thrust** themselves over.

Note: The throw is technically proper when the receiver is thrown straight over and back. I have found that beginning students learn better if they are allowed to throw to the side until the mechanics of throwing are done with ease.

DON'T FORGET

• **Over-Arm Grab:** Do not try to struggle to effect a re lease. Weaken your opponent before you attempt the finis techniques.

• **Gang-Attack Defense:** Take the initiative. Alterna your attacks so that neither opponent recovers sufficient to regain an advantage.

• **Circle Throw:** Do not stiff-leg your partner by straigh ening your right leg—he will fall on you if you do. Do n drag him onto the mat; guide him over. Once he is on h way over, let go. You will make it difficult for him to fa properly if you hang on.

The Seventeenth Day

Do everything you can to avoid fighting. If you are forced to fight, fight to win. Be alert when you are in a situation which has *any possibility* of danger. A lonely street offers more danger than a well-lit, busy thoroughfare. Certain neighborhoods in your town offer more potential danger than others—know where they are and behave accordingly.

LESSON OUTLINE

Review Instruction:

Falls No. 1, 2, 3, 7, 8
Fist-Fighting Defense:
  1. Hip-Throw Ending (p. 53)
  2. Swinging-Leg-Throw Ending (p. 80)
Close-in Fist-Fighting Defense—Block, Leap, Kick, and Choke (p. 149)
Knife Defense—Stabbing and Slashing Attacks (p. 136, 144)
Back-Grab Defense—Over Arms (p. 159)
Gang-Attack Defense—Front and Back (p. 160)
Sitting-Down Throw—Throwing and Receiving (p. 146)
Circle Throw—Throwing and Receiving (p. 162)

New Instruction:

Bent-Arm Lock—Rear
Knife Defense—Threat of Attack
Ninth Fall—Forward Fall from Knees
Sweeping-Foot Throw—Basic Steps (Position Only)

Don't Forget . . .

BENT–ARM LOCK—Rear

As previously noted, arm locks and similar techniques should be used for control of an annoying opponent, but not against a serious or dangerous attack. This arm lock, with its choke finish, is very effective.

1. The attacking partner, shown at the left, reaches out toward you. His intention may be to grab, push or pull, or to use any other annoying tactic. Slash into the nerve center of the reaching arm with your left hand.

2. After slashing, grip the cloth at his upper arm with your right hand, using an unnatural grip. Your left hand should remain in the place where it has slashed.

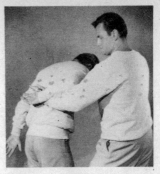

3. Pull forward with your right hand as you push the attacker's held arm back with your left hand. As you push and pull, take a deep step in with your left foot.

4. When the attacker's arm is pushed past his body, twist his arm up his back with your left arm, continuing your slight forward pull with your right hand.

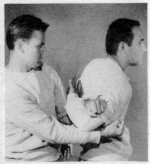

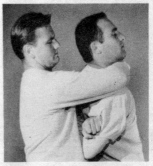

5. Step back with your right foot sliding your left arm between the attacker's back and the forearm of the captured arm as you step. Grip the cloth at his elbow with your left hand. Lock his held arm firmly between your left forearm and your body.

6. If necessary you may apply the choke finish to this arm lock by releasing your right-hand grip and pulling back against his neck with your right forearm. An alternate finish (not shown) is to maintain the arm lock with your left arm and pull back at his collar for good control. Maintain a strongly balanced "T" position.

KNIFE DEFENSE—Threat of Attack

In only one instance do I suggest a grappling type of defense against a knife—if the knife is being held stationary and you cannot leap back. If the attacker wants your money only, do not be foolhardy—give it up. If your life is being threatened, obviously you must make some attempt at defense. The essential preliminary to executing this defense is DISTRACTION.

1. The attacking partner simulates a knife threat with the knife held at your body. Use a rubber knife for training.

2. A slight hand movement which may serve to distract. Talking to your adversary, making eye movements, or slightly shifting your feet may also serve to distract. Distraction should be subtle, or you may startle him into using his weapon.

3. With your left hand, quickly grip his wrist and stiffen your arm. Turn your body away from the knife.

4. Keeping your arm stiff, poke your right hand into the attacker's eyes or throat.

5. When you have hurt the attacker, reach under his held arm with your right hand and take a firm grip.

6. To completely immobilize his knife hand, apply the Arm Lock with Thumb Release, which you learned on the Ninth Day. Only at this point should you take away his weapon.

NINTH FALL—Forward Fall from Knees

The advanced form of this fall is taught for safety only. It has no practical application in either sport or self-defense work. It can be used to avoid injury when you are pushed or tripped forward onto a hard surface. When you first practice this fall, execute it as shown in this lesson. The advanced form of the fall will be taught in a later lesson.

1. Assume the starting position shown here on a mat or on the grass.

2. Fall forward easily. Do not thrust yourself. As you lose your balance forward, bring your hands up in front of your face.

3. Do not allow your elbows to land first. Slap the mat with your full forearms and hands. Your hands should be directly in front of your face, elbows pointing out. Do not land on your wrists as this is exactly what you are trying to avoid. Your stomach should be off the ground.

SWEEPING–FOOT THROW—Basic Steps (Position Only)

This throw requires finesse and is one of the classic throws used in Sport Judo. With proper timing of the sweep and proper use of the arms for a twisting action, your adversary will go down with very little effort on your part. When you can execute this throw efficiently, you can apply it with good effect in street defense.

1. Start in the usual position for throwing practice. The thrower is shown at the right.

2. Rock your opponent with an arm motion so that all his weight is on one foot. Practice this until you have the feel of it. When you have him balanced well onto his left foot, turn your foot so that the entire bottom of it is ready to sweep at his ankle.

3. With the bottom of your left foot, sweep at his ankle until you have the proper timing. You will quickly realize that when you try to sweep too soon or too late, his foot will still be planted down too firmly for your sweep to be effective.

4. When you have learned to rock your opponent off balance and can time your sweeping action well, combine the rocking and sweeping action, and continue with a twist around and down with your arms to effect the throw. For the time being, merely take your partner well off balance and stop there.

DON'T FORGET

• Bent-Arm Lock—Rear: Be sure your opponent's arm is pushed well behind him before bending it. Lock his held arm in firmly so that he cannot wriggle free of your hold. Use any of the hand or foot blows to assist you in the action.

• Knife Threat: Do not attempt any action until you have distracted the attacker's attention from his weapon. Stiffen your arm when gripping his knife hand. Use foot blows in addition to hand blows. Take the knife away as soon as it is safe to do so.

• Ninth Fall: Fall easily. Do not thrust yourself down. Slap hard. Don't catch yourself on your wrists.

The Eighteenth Day

Practice the hand and foot blows in front of a mirror. When you are doing them properly, they will look good as well as feel right.

LESSON OUTLINE

Review Instruction:

Falls No. 1, 2, 3, 7, 9
Wrist-Grab Defense—All Four Types (p. 58, 67, 77, 85)
Grab Defense—Thumb Release and Arm Lock (p. 98)
Over-Arm Lock (p. 152)
Bent-Arm Lock—Rear (p. 166)
Knife Defense—Threat of Attack (p. 168)
Circle Throw—Throwing and Receiving (p. 162)
Sweeping-Foot Throw (Position Only) (p. 171)

New Instruction:

Fist-Fighting Defense—Parry and Take-down
Gun Defense—Back Attack
Sweeping-Foot Throw—Completion of Throw and Receiving
Judo Sparring Using Throws for Give-and-Take Practice—Free Use of All Basic Throws

Don't Forget . . .

FIST–FIGHTING DEFENSE—Parry and Take-down

Blocking is an ideal defense for close-in fist fighting. However, if your adversary is one or two steps away and punches from that distance, his blow will have his full body weight behind it and will be very difficult to block. In this situation parrying is an excellent defense because it will not oppose the attack but divert it. You should develop the ability to parry both right- and left-hand blows.

1. The attacking partner, shown at right, simulates a straight punch as the defending partner parries the attacking arm at the wrist. Simultaneously with the parry and without moving his feet, the defender should twist his body to the side out of fist range. Cup the parrying hand with the fingers together, and strike with the heel of the palm or with the palm (not the fingers) against the attacker's wrist or forearm. Parry with a sharp, snappy motion. Do not try to **push** his arm away.

2. By parrying the fist blow the defender should be able to turn the attacker somewhat to the side. Strike immediately with a hand blow into the middle area. Foot blows can also be used.

3. When his opponent is visibly weakened by hand and foot blows, the defender should step behind him, grip his collar with the right hand, and stamp into the back of his knee with the right foot. The simultaneous pulling back and kick into the knee will break the attacker's balance and the take-down can be made.

GUN DEFENSE—Back Attack

DO NOT ATTEMPT ANY DEFENSE against an armed attack if your adversary only wants to take money from you. If, however, your life is threatened and you cannot reason with or escape from your assailant, you must attempt a defense.

1. If you are threatened by some-one with a gun behind you, it is normal for you to glance around. As you do so, observe which hand is holding the gun. That is important in making the best defense.

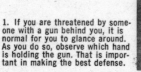

2. DISTRACT. Unless you use a subtle distracting motion, you may startle your adversary into shooting, or put him on guard. If you do not use a distracting motion, it is very dangerous to attempt your defense while his full attention is on his weapon. If the attacker reaches out to touch you, this is the time to make your defense, but if he does not, you may have to create your own distraction. The photo shows a slight finger wriggling to distract. Shuffling the feet can also distract.

3. Turn your body in the direction of the hand holding the gun. Because nine out of ten people are right-handed we show the gun held in the right hand. As you turn, snap your right hand back to strike at the attacker's forearm, diverting it from your body. The attacker's normal wrist action will not allow him to point the gun at you easily from this position.

4. & 5. Pivot in so that you are behind the gun and close to your adversary. Here you are momentarily safe. Capture his wrist between your forearm and upper arm to keep it immobile. You may then move in for stabbing finger blows to his eyes or windpipe (justified in this situation), or you may strike sharply with your forearm against his throat, as shown in Photo No. 5. If you pull sharply back on his held arm as you hit into his throat, it is possible to dislocate his elbow. Only when he is hurt and subdued should you take away his weapon.

SWEEPING-FOOT THROW—Completion of Throw and Receiving

1. When you have swept his foot and taken your partner off balance, you should twist the upper part of his body by pushing around and down with your right hand as you pull around and down with your left hand.

2. When your partner is on the way down, give a final thrust up with your sweeping foot and then put that foot down firmly to regain your balance. When the receiver feels both his feet leave the mat he should prepare to slap the ground.

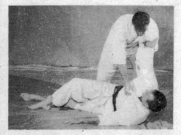

3. & 4. In beginning practice, you should maintain your hold on your opponent's sleeve and lapel to ease his fall. The receiver should finish in the position of the Second Fall. When both of you are more experienced, you will maintain your sleeve grip, but will release your grip on the lapel of the receiver, as in Photo No. 4. You should assume a strongly balanced "T" position at the completion of the throw.

JUDO SPARRING USING THROWS FOR GIVE–AND–TAKE PRACTICE—Free Use of All Basic Throws

To achieve a versatile use of the throws, you may practice in Judo sparring fashion. Keep in mind that throwing techniques are not absolutely necessary for strong street-defense. However, for those people who wish to develop throwing ability, or to prepare for advanced training in Judo, sparring is the best way to practice.

Sparring is the next step beyond give-and-take throwing from a standing position. Both you and your partner start in motion, holding on to each other in the usual manner for throwing practice. Sliding your feet almost as though you were dancing is the ideal way to move. Your arms should be constantly pulling and twisting your partner in the attempt to put him in a weak, off-balance position. Do not jerk or muscle your way into the throw. Gentle but constant guiding motions are better than strong-arm attempts. In Judo sparring you should not try to pit your strength against your partner's strength, but rather to test your skill. Your ability to react quickly, to recognize the throw which can be used in any of the off-balance positions, to execute the throws in good form—this is the essence of proper sparring practice.

DON'T FORGET

• Fist-Fighting Defense—Parry and Take-down: Duck your head out of your adversary's fist range and parry at his forearm. Do not parry at his upper arm.
• Gun Defense—Back Attack: Determine which hand holds the gun. DISTRACT. Go into action quickly. Do not try to hold him; hurt him.
• Sweeping-Foot Throw: Sweep at your opponent's ankle, not higher. Use the arm twist after the sweep, not before.

The Nineteenth Day

STRAIGHT–ARM LOCK AND FINGER PRESSURE

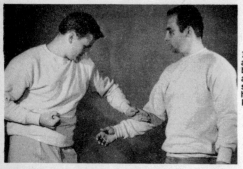

1. The attacking partner, sho[wn] at the right, reaches out to begin an annoying type of attack. The defending partner should strike at the nerve in his opponent's forearm. Use [a] left hand for this slash.

2. Follow the slash immediat[ely] by gripping the attacker's fingers with your right hand.

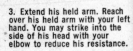

3. Extend his held arm. Reach over his held arm with your left hand. You may strike into the side of his head with your elbow to reduce his resistance.

4. Raise his held arm with your right hand, keeping it extended. Reach over and around with your left hand, and grip the cloth at your own chest.

5. Apply pressure by levering his held arm down over the bony part of your left forearm so that it presses against the nerve midway between his shoulder and elbow. Lift up with your left forearm as you pull down and back with your right hand.

GANG ATTACK DEFENSE—Front

Two or more opponents moving in to attack you from the front will ordinarily not expect any attack from you. If you are certain the attack is coming and you cannot avoid it move quickly to gain the advantage of surprise. You will only waste precious time if you plead or argue.

1. You are confronted by two or more opponents, coming at you at the same time. Though only two opponents are shown here, this method is practical against three or four opponents as well. At the first indication of danger, get into strong balance position preparatory to leaping.

2. Leap off to the outside of the attacking group.

3. Immediately kick at the closest opponent. A waist-high kick is shown in this photo. This is for training purposes only as it helps you to develop your ability to kick and regain your balance. In a fight, kick into the knee or shin.

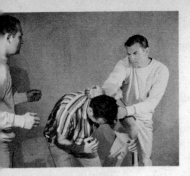

4. Follow with additional kicks and hand blows to weaken the same opponent further. The action described in these four photos must be done very quickly, as the second opponent will be moving in while this is happening.

5. Throw your weakened opponent into the nearest second opponent.

6. Leap off to the side of your next opponent and deliver kicks with force and speed. Follow this procedure, if necessary, against any other opponents. There is little likelihood that you will find it necessary to repeat this procedure more than once.

TENTH FALL—Forward Fall from Standing

This is an advanced form of the Ninth Fall. The finish is similar to that of the Ninth Fall, except that here the knees are off the mat.

1. In the starting position your feet are shoulder-width apart. Lose your balance forward and swing your arms up.

2. As you go forward, have your hands in position for slapping the mat.

3. Slap with the full length of your forearm from hand to elbow. Do not allow the elbow to touch first. Do not bend your hands so that your wrists make contact with the mat. Slap with your hands slightly cupped, your elbows pointing out to the side. Your hands should be directly in front of your face. Only your hands, forearms, and feet touch the mat at the finish of this fall.

KNEE-BLOCK THROW—Basic Steps (Position Only)

When an opponent is rushing toward you, you may be able to use this tripping type of throw without any preliminary striking techniques. Your opponent's balance should be broken well forward if you attempt this throw in Judo sparring practice.

1. You and your partner start in the usual starting position for a throw. The thrower is shown at the right.

2. The thrower should pull forward to break the receiver's balance. As the receiver comes forward, the thrower should sidestep with his right foot and get his left foot ready to trip.

3. The thrower continues pulling forward at the receiver and places the bottom of his left foot at the receiver's kneecap. When the receiver starts to go over, stop.

DON'T FORGET

• Straight-Arm Lock and Finger Pressure: Do not grip your opponent's fingers at the tips. Get a good, firm grip. The bony part of your left forearm must press at his arm well above the elbow. His upper arm should cross your forearm at a right angle.

• Gang Attack Defense—Front: Avoid being cornered. Leap to the outside of the group and attack the person closest to you; do not charge into the group. Concentrate on kicking rather than on hand blows. Throw the weakened opponent directly at the next nearest opponent, do not just fling him.

• Tenth Fall: Do not let your wrists or elbows hit first.

• Knee-Block Throw: As you sidestep, point your right foot at the receiver to give you the best balance. Both your knees should be slightly bent.

The Twentieth Day

The techniques which have been presented in this course are suitable for the majority of students. As an individual, however, you should feel free to be flexible in the application of what you have learned. Variations which seem helpful are totally acceptable and you can both learn a great deal and have fun by experimenting with different combinations of techniques.

LESSON OUTLINE

Review Instruction:

Falls No. 1, 2, 3, 7, 10
Straight-Arm Lock and Finger Pressure (p. 180)
Gang-Attack Defense—Front (p. 182)
Gun Defense—Back Attack (p. 175)
Stick or Club Defenses—Overhead Attack and Side Blow (p. 104, 128)
Front-Choke Defenses—No. 1 through 4 (p. 101, 110, 117, 126)
Sweeping-Foot Throw—Throwing and Receiving (p. 177)
Knee-Block Throw (Position Only) (p. 185)
Judo Sparring—Using Throws in Lessons 2 through 8

New Instruction:

Back-Choke Defense—Arm Grip
Gun Defense—Front Attack
Knee-Block Throw—Completion of Throw and Receiving
Karate Sparring—Using Slashes, Kicks, and Blocks at Nerve Centers for Give-and-Take Practice; Free Use of All Methods

Don't Forget . . .

BACK-CHOKE DEFENSE—Arm Grip

In the movies when the hero is choked from behind, he simply throws the villain over his shoulder. This is spectacular and unfortunately, completely impractical in a fight. It is very difficult to do such a throw without increasing the choking pressure when your balance is broken backward and there is a strong grip on your throat. The following defense, however, can be used.

1. Your partner simulates a choke attack. This attack is commonly called "mugging."

2. Relieve the pressure by gripping the attacker's choking arm with both hands. Grip with one hand at his wrist and with the other at the crook of his elbow. Turn your head into his elbow to relieve pressure at your windpipe. Jerk down on his choking arm with both your hands. This is done as one quick, snappy action.

3. After you have somewhat relieved the pressure, weaken your opponent by kicking into his shin and stamping onto his instep.

6. Pull your head free and twist his arm behind him and up.

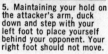

5. Maintaining your hold on the attacker's arm, duck down and step with your left foot to place yourself behind your opponent. Your right foot should not move.

4. When you have diverted his attention to the pain in his leg, jerk down again. This should completely break the choke. On the street, you should kick with force, scrape down his shin, and stamp down hard onto his instep. In training you should simulate this action to protect your partner.

7. Take a step back with your right foot to assume a strongly balanced "T" position. Maintain your grip at his wrist, keeping his arm twisted up. Release the grip with your right hand, and apply a choke with your forearm.

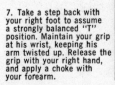

GUN DEFENSE—Front Attack

The introduction to the defense for an armed attack from behind applies to this situation as well. Do not attempt any defense against a gun threat if you can avoid it. Only if your life is threatened should you take action.

1. The attacker, shown at the right, threatens a gun attack from the front. His style of holding the gun is amateurish, indicating that you are probably dealing with someone who may be very nervous. Subtle distractions are, therefore, even more important because he could be startled into using his weapon if your movements are too obvious.

2. Shown here is a finger-wiggling distraction to divert his attention from his gun.

3. Your primary object is to stop the action of the gun. Using a swift, snappy movement reach with your left hand and grasp the gun and gun hand. Lock your fingers over the hammer because when it is immobilized the gun cannot be fired. Keep the muzzle pointed away from your body, and hold your left arm stiff and firm.

4. The instant that you have immobilized his weapon, begin your counter-attack using finger-stabbing blows into your assailant's eyes and throat.

5. After you have hurt your assailant, you may take away his gun. Keeping your left hand over the hammer, grasp his wrist.

6. Twist the assailant's held arm up and back, making certain that the muzzle of the gun remains pointed away from you.

7. When you have bent your assailant's arm well back, step in with your right foot to place it behind his right foot, breaking his balance backward.

8. You are now in a position to disarm your assailant and throw him. The weapon should be taken away before you execute the throw. You can also use the gun butt to strike into your assailant's face.

1. When the receiver's balance has been completely broken, use a sweeping motion of your foot to assist your arms and body which provide the principal action for this throw. Twist around and down to describe a circular movement with your arms. Your body follows the same movement.

2. When you begin practicing this throw, to ease the fall, maintain your grip on the receiver's sleeve and lapel throughout. The receiver should keep his grip at your sleeve throughout and finish with the Second Fall.

3. When you are more experienced, you should release the lapel grip and step back into a strong "T" position at the completion of the throw. You and your partner should maintain the sleeve grip throughout.

KARATE SPARRING—Using Slashes, Kicks, and Blocks at Nerve Centers for Give-and-Take Practice; Free Use of All Methods

You can now begin to practice basic Karate sparring. It is highly unlikely that you will encounter a Karate-trained opponent in a street fight. Therefore in your Karate sparring, you must not think of yourself as preparing to fight someone who has training similar to yours. As with Judo sparring, you are simply testing your ability to react, your versatility, and your technical skill.

You and your partner should take a fighting stance and move about as you attempt to deliver and block hand blows. Work slowly enough so that you retain control of your blows and can stop just before making contact. You should make contact in blocking only. As you develop skill in Karate sparring, you will be able to work faster and still pull your blows within an inch or two of landing. Avoid face or throat blows, and do not use kicks.

DON'T FORGET

• Back-Choke Defense: *First,* turn your head into the crook of the attacker's elbow to relieve the pressure. Stamp and kick before going into further action. Do not attempt hand blows before the choke is broken. Your hands are needed to stop the choking pressure.

• Gun Defense—Front Attack: Under no circumstance attempt any action until you have taken the attacker's attention from his weapon; then move quickly. Once you have grasped his hand and gun, keep the muzzle pointed away from you. Do not take the gun away until after you have hurt him.

• Knee-Block Throw: Do not *kick* your partner's knee; place your foot there and use a sweeping action.

The Twenty-First Day

The success of your training can be measured to a great extent by how *infrequently you will need to use the techniques you have learned*. With the confidence of your training to back you up, you will discover that you have much greater control of situations which might previously have resulted in physical violence. Even the tone of your voice will clearly indicate that you do not wish to fight, but that you are quite prepared if necessary to fight and *win*. If an obnoxious person raises his voice, lower yours. Remember that there are many kinds of courage. When you can accept the idea of walking away from a fight, you have achieved a discipline which adds to your character. Knowing that you could, if necessary, subdue an adversary, you may decline to do so with dignity whenever you have that opportunity. Never retaliate beyond the need of the situation. Defend yourself with honor.

LESSON OUTLINE

Review Instruction:

> Falls No. 1 through 10
> Back-Choke Defense—Arm Grip (p. 188)
> Gun Defense—Front and Back Attacks (p. 175, 190)
> Gang-Attack Defense—Front Only and Front and Back (p. 160, 182)
> Fist-Fighting Defenses—Vary the Attacks and Try Various Defenses
> Judo Sparring—Using All Throws Learned
> Karate Sparring—Using All Methods from "Where and How to Strike" Section

New Instruction:

> Fist-Fighting Defense—Close-In Attack—Kick, Lock, and Spin
> Gang-Attack Defense—Arm Pin, Front and Back

Don't Forget . . .

FIST–FIGHTING DEFENSE: CLOSE–IN ATTACK—Kick, Lock, and Spin

1. The attacking partner, shown at the right, simulates a close-in fist attack.

2. As circumstances do not allow you to leap out of range of his fist, block his blow outward.

3. Immediately block the other arm whether or not it is striking. In a fight you would lose time if you were to wait for his second blow and then block it. In your training, always assume there will be a follow-up blow, and be prepared to block it.

4. Grip the cloth at both the attacker's elbows or his elbows themselves, and thrust his arms out. Keep your arms rigid. This will immobilize his arms for a moment so that you may continue your defense.

5. & 6. Kick your adversary as many times as needed to hurt him. Use various kinds of kicks—the inside and outside edge-of-the-shoe kicks, and the toe, bottom, and heel kicks. Slash, stamp, scrape, etc. Alternate your right and left foot for kicking so that he will be confused as well as hurt.

7. Twist your adversary sharply so that his back is toward you.

8. Continue with hand and foot blows until your opponent is completely subdued.

GANG–ATTACK DEFENSE—Arm Pin, Front and Back

1. You are held from behind by one member of a gang, while another threatens to attack.

2. Using the opponent behind for support, kick at the other attacker. In training practice, kick high; in a fight you should kick both high and low, wherever an opening appears.

3. & 4. When you have hurt the opponent in front of you, strike with back kicks and slashes at the person holding you. This defense should weaken the person holding you sufficiently to allow your escape, as shown in the photo on the right. You can then retaliate with hand blows.

5. When you are completely free, leap off to the side and be ready to use kicks against either opponent.

DON'T FORGET

• **Fist-Fighting Defense:** Grip the cloth at the attacker's *elbows*, or the elbows themselves, and lock his arms out with your arms rigid. Start your kicking before he can escape.

• **Gang-Attack Defense:** Since the opponent holding you is not hurting you, but only restraining you, kick to the front first.

Introduction to Teaching Women and Children

Now that you have finished this home-study course, you have learned considerably more than you need to know for effective self-defense.

It is normal for students to favor some of the techniques over others. Since we all have different types of bodies and different ways of using them for physical action, it is logical that we should find some techniques better suited to our personal style than others. If you have achieved real skill in only half of the defenses in the course, you have a good reserve for practical use.

You may continue beyond the course, practicing the defenses for exercise, coordination, and body toning. Perhaps the best method of increasing your skill is to instruct a new partner. This will further solidify your knowledge and give you, in addition, the marvelous satisfaction of teaching.

If you continue to practice with your original partner, you may improvise combinations of defenses based on your favorite techniques and practice for speed and precision.

Instructing a woman or a child is different from instructing or practicing with a new male partner. With a new male partner, patience is important, but you must develop new skills (and extraordinary patience) if you are to be a good instructor for a woman or a child. In fact, the successful training of a woman or a child can be taken as an indication of your ability to teach well and is an accomplishment of which you may be proud.

In the following sections you will find special material which will help you in this type of instruction.

How to Teach
Self-Defense
to a Child

PATIENCE, TEACHER: Whether or not you have achieved a high degree of proficiency in self-defense skills, you can teach your child. The ability to teach does not necessarily accompany the ability to perform the skill which is being taught. There are many professional football and basketball coaches who cannot play the games nearly as well as the athletes they are instructing and there are music teachers who cannot perform as well as their students. It is possible therefore for you to teach your child before you have become an expert in the unarmed arts yourself.

Understanding and patience will be your most important tools in teaching successfully. Although the learning process requires patience, teaching requires even greater patience and a constant attempt by the teacher to understand the student's problems and to overcome them.

CONFIDENCE AND MORAL SUPPORT FOR THE PEACEABLE CHILD

Surprisingly the child who benefits most from learning Judo-Karate self-defense is the child who is not physically aggressive and who shys away from fighting for it is to this child that the confidence and self-esteem that he gains can be most important. The child who is either afraid to defend himself or physically unable to suffers intensely when he is forced to run from a fight or lose it. The small boy has obvious disadvantages; however, even the tall, timid boy is constantly put upon by other children who know his weakness. Such a child is frequently doubly ashamed of himself —once for the humiliation he suffers at the hands of other youngsters, and again for not coming up to what he feels are your standards.

Unfortunately the society in which we live has a peculiar

double standard relating to physical violence. At school, at church, in books we teach our children that fighting is bad; however, the glorification of violence which our children see on TV and in movies, cartoons, and "comic" books must outweigh wiser guidance. The boy who wants to avoid fighting needs stronger moral support than we give him to have the confidence of having a principled position. As intelligent adults, we do not admire men whose only one response to an argument is a punch in the nose. At the same time we pity the man whose only response to a punch in the nose is to run away. It is important that you make it clear to your child that you do not want him to be an aggressive, bullying person; however every child should be able to stop an attack, and, if necessary, subdue his adversary. With that ability to give him confidence, your child may even decline to fight and do so with dignity.

There are children who find fighting so repugnant that although they can learn to stop an attack, they will not retaliate. Such children must not be forced to push beyond their natural inclination. Happily, stopping the attack is very often sufficient to put an end to bullying.

ENCOURAGEMENT IS IMPORTANT

Encourage the child throughout the training, and remember that if he has difficulty in learning, your encouragement is needed all the more. Anyone can learn the techniques in this course. Mentally retarded children and physically handicapped children (including blind children), as well as very bright children with serious problems of mind-body coordination have mastered them. Doctors and teachers report that these children have gained great advantages from their training, whether they have achieved a high degree of proficiency or have mastered only a few simple techniques for limited use. Whatever the problem confronting the child whom you wish to teach, he can learn if you are sufficiently patient and encouraging.

Always phrase your instruction in positive terms. Avoid saying, "That is wrong." Say, instead, "The proper way to do that . . ." You may encourage the child by praising effort or improvement but do not praise falsely because this will undermine your position of authority. Avoid a critical tone, and make corrections in a matter-of-fact manner.

THE SECRET WEAPON

At the beginning of the training, especially, you must make the child understand that he is not to "play" with his new knowledge and show off to other children what he has learned. If he tries it too soon, he may not succeed and will lose confidence in the practicality of his techniques. Explain that what he is learning is his "secret weapon" to be used when needed. If he gives away the secret, he will lose the advantage of surprise in making his defense.

KICKING IS JUSTIFIED FOR DEFENSE

The accusation of being a "poor sport" is one which children greatly fear. In justifying the use of kicking for street defense it is necessary to point out the fact that there are no "Queensberry rules" in street fighting. Sporting rules apply to contests which are controlled and supervised, not to bullying and vicious attacks. A bully has violated every concept of sportsmanship when he attacks an unwilling and seemingly helpless person, and he is not entitled to the protection of the rules he has ignored.

TEACHING HINTS

It is best to give a child verbal instructions rather than demonstrating with your hands. If the child has come to dislike physical contact, he will not respond well to being handled while he is trying to learn. If you need to move him into position, use a firm, but not rough, action.

Observe all the Safety Rules as given in the Preliminary Instruction. A very timid child should be allowed to inflict some slight pain on his partner or instructor to indicate to him that the techniques are effective. As he gains confidence, he will be able to take slight pain himself, but you must be very careful not to let him be hurt by careless pressure in the beginning or you will create a serious resistance to further training.

Usually you can judge a child's progress by his manner of gripping. At the start of the training, if he is instructed to grip his partner, he is likely to do so with a rigid, inflexible hold, or with a soft, lifeless hand. As he gains confidence, he will be able to use a firm, controlled grip. Other indications of confidence are a strongly balanced stance and controlled, strong simulated blows.

It is not required that you train a child in a Judo or Karate suit, but it does add a feeling of authenticity to the training and is a psychological aid if he has to change into a uniform.

WHAT TO TEACH A CHILD

Your own judgment will have to determine what is suitable for your child to learn. The circumstances of his everyday encounters and his aptitude and his preferences of techniques must be taken into account. The special section of work for children in this chapter is based on common situations which are encountered by children more often than by adults. In addition to these special techniques, you should take the child slowly through all the lessons in this course, eliminating those things which your good sense tells you are not necessary. Be sure to teach only the striking areas and methods of striking which are covered in this section for children.

Unless your child demonstrates a higher degree of aptitude, you should be satisfied to teach him one or two simple arm locks. The falls are useful for safety, but need not be learned for good street defense. Concentrate on a few throws, emphasizing a front and a back tripping-type throw for practical use. Very timid or fearful children should not be thrown, or should be thrown only after they have made good progress in their training and have demonstrated a willingness to learn how to receive.

WHERE AND HOW TO STRIKE

Teaching a limited number of techniques to a child is better than trying to teach him many techniques. Most situations with which a boy must deal can be handled if he knows a few striking methods with his hands and feet and has learned a dozen striking areas from the front and a half-dozen from the rear. The Ways to Strike have been chosen because they are the most versatile, and children can learn them easily. The Places to Strike have been chosen because a child can hit with full force and great effectiveness at these areas without danger of serious or permanent injury.

STRIKING METHODS: Hand Blows. Teach the side-of-the-hand blow, the extended-knuckle blow, the heel-of-the-palm blow and the elbow blow. Practice using first one hand and then the other. Efficiency will be achieved when both hands can be used equally well. Practice the four types of blows against the suspended ball for coordination and against the bag for full release of power. In practice with his partner, the child should only simulate the blows and barely make contact.

WHERE TO STRIKE: Teach *only* these areas for striking. They are sufficient for children.

> *Front:* Under ear, side of neck, neck muscle (do not teach windpipe), shoulder muscle, elbow, forearm, wrist, back of hand, under last rib, straight into stomach (do not teach upward blow into stomach), upper thigh, lower thigh, shin, ankle, instep. *Rear:* Side of neck, shoulder muscle, thigh, calf, ankle.

As you teach, let the child try the various types of blows at all the striking areas to find the ones which work best for him. Emphasize striking at the forearm nerve center and the shoulder muscle.

KICKING METHODS: Use the bottom, edges, and heel of the shoe. If barefoot, work with the bottom of the foot using the heel or ball of the foot. Emphasize kicks to the shin. Practice coordination and balance by kicking at the suspended ball. Practice full power kicks (and return to balance) by kicking at the bag.

SPECIFIC DEFENSES FOR CHILDREN

HEADLOCK: Shown in photo is the front headlock. The same defense as is shown here can be easily used against a rear headlock, or for a front bearhug. When grabbed, the defender should avoid trying to struggle or wriggle free. We always assume that the bully is larger than the boy defending; therefore, strength will not solve the problem. The defender should strike with the extended knuckle into one or both sides of the opponent, striking just under the last rib. It is also possible to strike into the thigh with extended knuckles. If this is not enough to obtain release, he should kick into the attacker's shin or stamp down on his instep.

After effecting his release, the defender should stand up straight, and step back out of range of the opponent's fists. He should be alert for a second attack and be prepared to kick and slash in retaliation if necessary.

HAIR-PULLING FROM THE REAR: When the opponent pulls hair, photo (left), the defender should put both hands on the top of the pulling hand and press down. This will relieve the pain. Keeping the hands pressed down, he should then kick back into the attacker's shin, photo (right), to divert his attention from the hair pulling. At this point it is possible to take the pulling hand away and turn to face the attacker, ready to continue the defense, if necessary. If the hair-pulling hand is held while the turn is done, it is simple to continue with a wrist lock or armlock.

GRABBING FROM THE REAR: If the opponent attacks from the rear, regardless of specific intent (he may be punching the shoulder or trying to pull a notebook away or slapping or grabbing from the back), the simultaneous slash and kick is the best defense, as in photo. Only the head needs to be turned so that the opponent can be seen. The first kick may be enough to change the opponent's mind about attacking, but one should always be alert for further action. After the kick and slash retaliation, the defender should turn to face the aggressor and be ready to continue his defense if needed.

FIST–FIGHTING: Sometimes it is possible to stop a fist-fighting attack if the defending boy assumes a Judo-Karate fighting stance, as shown in photo (left). A bully is not eager to take on someone who may hurt him. Photo (right) shows how to block both arms if fist blows are attempted. It is best to block both arms even though the opponent may hit with only a single blow. If this does not completely stop the attack, kicking and slashing several times will.

DEFENSES FROM THE GROUND

BASIC RULE: If the defending boy has fallen or has been pushed and finds himself on the ground with an opponent moving in to strike, he should **remain on the ground as long as the opponent is within kicking or striking range.** Keeping his head off the ground, the arms and hands should be used to position the body so that the opponent is never allowed to get near the head, as shown in photo. The defender's feet should be aimed at the attacker. If the attacker tries to move around to the side, the defender should pivot on the small of his back, pushing with his hands, so that his feet remain pointed at the attacker. The defender should kick with force at his adversary's shins and knees. The kicking action should be continued until the attacker is hurt or retreats. The defender should not get up while the attacker is still close to him and should always get up facing his opponent. Under no circumstance should he turn his back while his opponent is within striking range. It is always best to be prepared for further kicks and slashes if necessary.

SITTING-ON-CHEST HOLDDOWN: To repeat, we always expect that the bully will be larger than the defending boy. Therefore, to attempt to wiggle or struggle out of this hold is simply a waste of energy. Photo (left) shows the basic holddown and the first step of the defense: the legs are drawn up as far as possible, and there is a sudden bridging of the back. These actions should be accompanied by a loud yell shouted into the opponent's face. The bridging, which throws the opponent's weight forward and the yelling, which startles him, should be done simultaneously. The next step, photo (right), is done without hesitation. When the defender has brought the opponent forward by the bridging action, he should push with one foot as he twists his whole body to the left (in this photo the right foot is pushing), throwing the attacker off to the side. When the attacker has been thrown off, his feet should be pushed away immediately so that he cannot kick, and the defender should slide himself around to the attacker's head where he will be in a good position to slash at his arms and neck if necessary. The defender should get up as soon as he is completely free.

SITTING-ON-BACK HOLDDOWN: Photo (above, left) shows the opponent sitting on the back of the defending boy with the defender's arms pinned back. Again, energy should not be wasted in trying to struggle or wiggle free. With his free hand, the defender should reach over and push at the captured hand, as in photo (above). At the same time, he should roll slightly to the right side. The opponent will normally resist that motion by leaning to the opposite side. Using the attacker's body motion to the left side, the defender should pull his right foot up, push with the bottom of his right foot as he twists his entire body suddenly to throw the attacker off his back, as in photo (left). As he twists the defender should yell and when he is free, he should immediately slide away, getting to his feet when he is out of striking range.

How to Teach Self-Defense to a Woman

Using no greater strength than she does every day for her household work a woman can learn to defend herself. Only a small assortment of Judo-Karate techniques is necessary for self-defense, but the method of training and the selection of techniques are of utmost importance.

Attacks on women are usually made by men who do not expect any kind of skilled defense. The unprepared woman will struggle, pull hair, or beat her fists against the attacker's chest in a vain effort to defend herself. The attempt to struggle will have no effect—the attacker must be supposed to have greater strength than the woman. Pulling hair has some effect, but not enough to stop a determined man and the beating of fists on his chest is a total waste of energy.

However, a "masher" can easily be discouraged. A knuckle to the back of his hand, a simple wrist lock, stepping on his instep with high heels—any of these will work wonders. With a small selection of hand and foot blows and a knowledge of a few nerve centers, a woman is well prepared to deal with an annoying man.

THE BEHAVIOR OF CONFIDENCE

Fright, which is due to a total lack of preparedness, can cause immobility. Proper training should give a woman the composure which will allow her judgment to function even in times of crisis. The confidence which can be gained from training can by itself avert an attack as the way in which a woman walks on the street can indicate her state of mind. There is no more terrifying situation for a woman than to imagine that she is in danger and yet not have the courage to look. She finds herself on a lonely street, hears footsteps or shuffling behind her, and dares not turn around. Because she has no way of contending with danger, she is afraid to face it and therefore leaves herself in the most vulnerable possible position.

When teaching a woman, your first instruction should be: never turn your back on an adversary! If danger is suspected, turn to face it. That very act may avert an attack.

When she turns around to look, she may find one of these things to be true:

1. There is a person behind her, but it is quite obviously someone who just happens to be going in the same direction. (An abnormally fearful person will see danger in any situation; a reasonable person is capable of making a judgment about what constitutes danger and what does not.)

2. There is someone behind her whose manner or appearance causes enough suspicion of danger that she must be alert. By knowing this beforehand she has the advantage of a precious moment in which to plan her action. *Anything* she does is better than nothing. She may suddenly cross the street and start walking in the opposite direction. Or she may go to a place where there is a light showing and ask for admission—even if it is a private house. If she is carrying a purse, she should open it and put her hand inside to give the impression that she is carrying a weapon. If there is danger, and she allows herself to be attacked from the rear, a woman has placed herself in the worst possible position to make a defense. However, even in this situation she should be trained to defend herself.

THE PURSE ARSENAL

In every woman's purse there is a little arsenal of common articles which may be used for defense. Lipstick, a comb, a compact—are likely to be in a woman's purse at all times. Let her practice hitting with any of these articles. Random striking out will not be nearly so effective as one or two blows aimed at the proper spot, and therefore this practice should be done at specific striking areas. Other weapons available in her purse may include a fingernail file, a mirror or a pen. In the event of serious deadly attack, if a woman can put her hands on such an important weapon and strike into the throat or eyes she may save her life. It is important to make a very clear distinction between the kinds of blows which may be used for defense against an annoying opponent and against one who is vicious or violent.

WHAT TO WEAR FOR INSTRUCTION

Casual, comfortable clothes should be worn by the woman student when her training is started. As she makes progress, she should alternate training periods in these clothes and in her street wear. The kind of shoes she wears most often for street dress should be worn for kicking practice. High heels are an excellent aid to kicking, and special practice should be done if this is the type of shoe she wears frequently. Use the suspended ball for practice in coordination and balance. Low kicks, at knee-height and at the shin, are best for practical use. If the woman has great difficulty learning to kick with her high-heeled shoes, train her to take her shoes off at the first indication of danger. She can then use the shoe to good advantage as a hand weapon.

WHAT TO TEACH WOMEN

As a woman does not need to know a great many techniques, it is best to teach her a limited number and let her achieve proficiency in them. Teach her the methods of striking and kicking as outlined in the children's section. Add to that the stabbing finger blows into the eyes and the side-of-the-hand blow across the windpipe, for use in defense of her life.

In choosing the techniques which she should learn, you should be guided by her preference and her ability to learn. There is a wide variation in these matters, and you must approach this without any preconceptions. Do not compel your woman student to learn the techniques most favored by you. Go through the course, and offer her all the techniques in an introductory fashion. Skip those which she does not like, and concentrate on those which she prefers. Do not overwhelm her by moving too quickly or insisting that she learn too much. She is much better prepared to face danger if she knows six things well than if she has half-learned sixty techniques.

YELL!

You have read many newspaper accounts which say ". . . neighbors were attracted to the scene by the screams . . ." As an aid in making her defense, and as a defense measure above, yelling is of particular importance to your woman student. In your training, place a heavy emphasis on yelling as blows are practiced.

Struggling or pushing is the usual "defense" made by a woman who has had no training. Her adversary who is larger, has greater strength and more weight making this action a waste of energy.

In exactly the same situation, using self-defense techniques a woman may effectively defend herself with hand and foot blows. Even a minimum training program will greatly develop her ability.

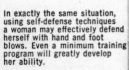

An arm lock and a wrist hold of her choice should be part of the training. These should be taught not for use against a vicious attack, but as handy control techniques. An insistent man, perhaps drunk, who is not amenable to reason, may be handled in this manner.

Using a small number of techniques to best advantage, a woman can stop an attack, retaliate, and even take her opponent down, if necessary. The throws best suited for use by women are the front tripping-type throw or the back throws shown here. Throwing should be preceded by hand and foot blows to distract and weaken the attacker.

A defense against a back choke using the most simple, effective techniques—the one-finger grip to effect release, followed by an elbow blow and a stamp on the instep.

Fourth Progress Test

1. Although it is preferable to avoid grappling with a knife attacker, and to use a leap-and-kick defense instead, you can grip the knife hand:
    - A. When the knife is stabbing straight in.
    - B. When you are sure the knife is dull.
    - C. When the knife is stationary.
2. A method of testing your ability to react, and your technical skill as well, is:
    - A. Get into a fight.
    - B. Practice with your partner under conditions of street fighting.
    - C. Practice Judo and Karate sparring.
3. When being choked, your first action should be to:
    - A. Relieve the choking pressure.
    - B. Wound your adversary.
    - C. Distract your opponent.
4. The final and most useful aim of all your training is:
    - A. Lightning-fast reactions.
    - B. Knowing that you can defend yourself and having the confidence which allows you to avoid a fight whenever possible.
    - C. The ability to defend from any position.
5. The most important techniques to learn are:
    - A. High kicking.
    - B. A variety of those you prefer.
    - C. Throwing and take-downs.

6. You should never make a defense against an armed attack unless your life is threatened. If you are required to defend yourself, your actual defense must always be preceded by:
    A. A verbal threat.
    B. Pretense of a fist attack.
    C. Distraction.
7. The most effective self-defense method is:
    A. A combination of techniques from all the arts.
    B. Karate.
    C. Aikido-Yawara.
8. In order to teach a child, you must first:
    A. Overcome his cowardice.
    B. Assure him of your confidence in him.
    C. Teach him to tolerate physical pain.
9. The techniques which you should teach a child are:
    A. Everything he is able to learn.
    B. Only the mildest defenses.
    C. A selection of techniques based on his ability and appropriate to his need.
10. In addition to kicking and striking, a woman should learn about:
    A. The purse arsenal.
    B. Sport Judo.
    C. Karate sparring.

Answers on page 224.

Appendix

FRONT

STRIKING AREA

(The letters indicate striking areas on drawing at right.)
(Numbers indicate the degree of pain, resulting from blows to the area. See key at lower right.)

	light blow	medium blow	heavy blow
a. Temple	3	4	5
b. Nose	2	3	4
c. Ear	1	2	3
d. Under jaw	1	2	3
e. Neck muscle	1	2	3
f. Side of neck	2	3	4
g. Windpipe (Adam's apple)	3	4	5
h. Shoulder muscle	1	2	3
i. Hollow of throat	3	4	5
j. Solar plexus	2	3	4, 5
k. Side, just below last rib	1	2	3
l. Lower abdomen	2	3	4, 5
m. Elbow joint, inside	1	2	3
n. Forearm	1	2	3
o. Wrist	1	2	3
p. Back of hand	1	2	3
q. Fingers	1	2	3
r. Upper and lower thigh	1	2	3
s. Knee	2	3	4
t. Shin	2	3	4
u. Ankle	1	2	3
v. Instep	1	2	3

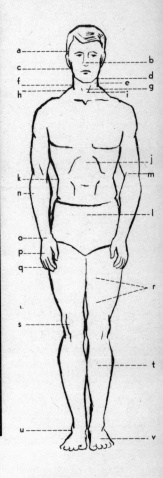

O STRIKE

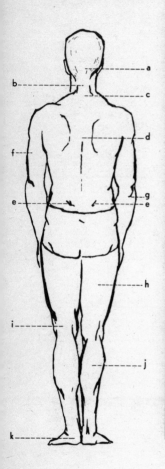

BACK

STRIKING AREA

(The letters indicate striking areas on drawing at left.)
(Numbers indicate the degree of pain, resulting from blows to the area. See key below.)

	light blow	medium blow	heavy blow
a. Base of skull	3	4	5
b. Center of neck	2	3	4
c. 7th vertebra (at base of neck)	3	4	5
d. Back (center, between shoulder blades)	2	3	4
e. Kidney	3	4	5
f. Back of arm	1	2	3
g. Back of elbow joint	1	2	3
h. Back of upper leg	1	2	3
i. Back of knee	1	2	3
j. Calf	1	2	3
k. Tendon (Achilles' heel)	1	2	3

KEY TO DEGREE OF PAIN

1. Moderate pain.
2. Sharp pain.
3. Stunning and/or numbing. Stunning may result from blows in the head and neck area. It interferes seriously with adversary's ability to react. Numbing prevents use of limbs for periods from several seconds up to several hours.
4. Temporary paralysis or unconsciousness. Temporary paralysis can last for minutes or hours.
5. Severe injury, possible permanent injury, or fatality. This degree of retaliation is justified only in the face of a vicious attack in which your life is endangered.

WHERE TO STRIKE

Front

Back

(*Also see chart on page 220.*)

HOW TO STRIKE

The page number given here will tell you where to find the instruction in the sections "HOW AND WHERE TO STRIKE." The page numbers in parenthesis will tell you where to find *additional* examples of this type of striking method in the text.

Hand and Arm Blows

Foot Blows

DEFENSES

Back Attacks

Fist fighting defenses

Front choke defenses

Gang attack defenses

ANSWERS TO PROGRESS TESTS

First Progress Test

1. B.
2. C.
3. A.
4. A.
5. B.
6. C.
7. C.
8. A.
9. B.
10. A.

Second Progress Test

1. A.
2. B.
3. A.
4. C.
5. B.
6. C.
7. C.
8. B.
9. A.
10. C.

Third Progress Test

1. B.
2. A.
3. B.
4. C.
5. B.
6. A.
7. B.
8. C.
9. C.
10. A.

Fourth Progress Test

1. C.
2. C.
3. A.
4. B.
5. B.
6. C.
7. A.
8. B.
9. C.
10. A.